CREA . _

YOUR OWN

GODDESS

CREATE
YOUR OWN
GODDESS

SHEENA BARNES & FRAN HAZELTON

CONNECTIONS
BOOK PUBLISHING

Especially for Danya Bradley-Barnes and Katrina Maven-Hazelton

A CONNECTIONS EDITION
This edition published in Great Britain in 2001 by
Connections Book Publishing Limited
St Chad's House, 148 King's Cross Road
London WC1X 9DH

British Library Cataloguing-in-Publication data available on request

ISBN: 1-85906-063-3

10 9 8 7 6 5 4 3 2 1

Phototypeset in Arrus BT and DaVinci on AppleMacintosh in QuarkXPress
Origination by Bright Arts, Singapore
Printed and produced by Hung Hing Offset Printing Co., Ltd
Manufactured in China

*Note: The clay in this kit is packed in airtight wrapping. If, however, it has dried
out slightly during storage, place in a bowl of water overnight. Remove from water
and the clay should be ready to use again.*

*The clay included in this kit is non-toxic. However, it is advisable to keep it out of
reach of young children, because it should not be eaten. Wash hands with soap and
water after use. If the clay gets in your eyes or mouth, wash out thoroughly with
water. If irritation occurs, seek medical attention.*

Contents

The Goddesses

Foreword

This book-kit is the fruit of a long conversation between us which took place in a 'hammam' or Turkish baths in London over many months. Because we both liked water, swimming and steaming we would meet to relax and have a giggle in the Porchester Spa, Bayswater, which is an oasis of stillness amidst the desert storm of stressful city life.

Here, surrounded by other disrobed women of various shapes, sizes, ages and nationalities, we discovered we had lots to talk about as we rested on loungers sipping lemon and ginger tea after a prolonged hot sweat in the steam room or a soothing soak in the jacuzzi.

We had first met in a women's group which provided mutual support and encouragement by sharing feelings, nurturing trust and helping each other escape from restrictive predicaments, accept losses, heal wounds and go on with life anew.

Fran had graduated in politics, philosophy and economics, and then modern Middle Eastern studies. She became a campaigner for human rights in Iraq. A trip to Iraqi Kurdistan as an election observer after the Gulf War sparked in her a deep and abiding fascination with Mesopotamian mythology, particularly the myths of the goddess Inana or Ishtar.

Sheena graduated in fine art and then theology. She was one of the first women to qualify as a Reverend in the 450-year-old Church of England. Her eyes were opened to other traditions by a trip to India, where art and religion are not separate and goddess-worship is widespread. When she returned, she began to express her spirituality through her paintings which are regularly exhibited in England and Europe.

Sheena also wanted to combine art with the search for useful archetypes for women in the world religions, so she began organizing 'Create Your Own Goddess' workshops. These were always great fun and full of laughter as participants discovered the joy and satisfaction of engaging their hands, eyes, hearts and minds in the art of female spirituality, ancient and modern.

The purpose of this book-kit is to spread that joy and satisfaction.

Sheena's paintings can be seen on her website www.ycta.net/sheena

Introduction

*A*round the planet, from prehistoric times to the present day, people have made sacred female figurines. You can now experience the enjoyment and deep satisfaction of this art form. Transcend your own place and time to put yourself in touch with other cultures, ancient and modern. Express artistically the eternal continuities of female spirituality. Find and celebrate the divine in yourself by creating your own goddess. You can make a good goddess-figure even if you are a beginner with clay modelling. Experts can explore and develop the art form. You can create your own goddess alone, with a relative or friend, in a group, or at a workshop. However you do it, you will be participating in an activity as old and as worldwide as humankind.

Choosing Your Goddess

*B*efore deciding which goddess you would like to make, take a look through this book to see which one most inspires you. You could choose a figurine from another time or place you feel close to. Perhaps ancient Egypt or Celtic England, for example?

Would you prefer a two-dimensional representation like the Sacred Trio relief? Or a three-dimensional figurine like the great goddess Isis or the Sleeping Lady of Malta?

What is going on in your life? If you are pregnant, Akua'ba might be for you. If you seek tranquillity, turn to the Cycladic Grave Figure. For a stronger awareness of female power see the Goddess of Growth. For ancient strength, try the Bird-headed Snake Goddess from Egypt. For ancient wisdom, see the Venus of Laussel. Each has its own attraction and power.

The instructions for each goddess are preceeded by a star rating for difficulty. One star is easy, two moderate and three challenging. You should allow at least one hour to make your goddess and some of the more difficult figurines may take up to three hours. It is important that you work at your own pace. Mark your goddess with your own intials and the date to make it personal to you.

Meditation and Creativity

Each goddess is accompanied by a meditation or poem. You may choose to record this and listen to it as you make your goddess. You could ask a friend to read it aloud. Building your own altar (see pages 10–14) allows you to further this contemplative process and reap the rewards of your own creativity.

The act of creation is a process inspired by the desire to discover the divine, make visible the invisible, make known the unknown and give form to the formless. As you create, remind yourself of your predecessors – those who originally created the figurine that inspires the goddess you are modelling – and empathize with them.

Each goddess is a personal interpretation of the original. That is her power. The photographs of each goddess made by different people in this book show the great variety and individuality which everyone brings to the creative process.

Healing Inspiration

As you honour the creativity of those who made the goddesses in this book – both in recent years and long ago – acknowledge that their creativity has been the spark to ignite yours. Feel the healing power of that spark as you leave behind anxiety, frustration and sadness to concentrate on your creative work. Allow yourself to experience the sacredness of the female and welcome its presence. Let the creation of your goddess be a synthesis of your feelings, mood, and sense of yourself.

Creating your own goddess should be a relaxing and restorative process. Whatever you put into the making of your goddess will look back at you and reward you when you meditate on her in the future.

As time passes and you experience changes in your life, you may wish to make new goddesses to reflect those changes within yourself. The figures in this book represent all ages and situations. Gain further inspiration and enjoy your own creativity.

Making an Altar

Designating a sacred place and making an altar may not be something you are familiar with. It is often thought of as a Hindu practice, seen with the pathway icons of India, although other faiths make personal altars too. But when Diana, Princess of Wales was killed in a car crash in France, the royal parks of London were filled with shrines to her. They were instinctively made by a shocked and grieving public, who placed her framed photographs at the foot of trees, decorated lawns and railings with flowers, lit candles, wrote poems and wept. Very few of them were Hindus.

Shrines and altars are seen in other areas of our everyday lives, although we may not immediately recognize them as such. Teenagers have shrines in their bedrooms to stars of the silver screen, pop music or sport. In the workplace executives put photographs on their desks of their family, perhaps beside a pot plant, as a reminder of what they hold sacred and treasure spiritually.

The purpose of creating an altar is to make a place where you can focus on your finished goddess and meditate with her. It does not correlate to any one set of religious beliefs and is based on the premise that contemplation can enrich our lives.

Creating Your Altar

When deciding where to set up your altar, you need to consider whether you have space to make it a permanent feature in your home, or whether you would prefer something which can be set up whenever you need it and put away again quickly and easily. You will

also need to think about whether you wish to make an elaborate altar (see pages 12–13), or whether a simple focus for meditation as illustrated opposite (using only a piece of fabric, your goddess and a candle) is more to your taste. It can be as elaborate or as simple as you like. As a general rule, your altar should always be personal to you.

It could be permanently set up in a cupboard with doors which can be closed, so it is kept from general view. Or it could be on display on a window ledge or kitchen shelf. Perhaps it could be on the mantlepiece in the living room, or in your bathroom. It could just as easily be in the garden or on your desk beside your computer as you work. Perhaps your bedroom seems to be the most obvious place to put an altar; a place of calm and quiet.

Your altar should designate a sacred place. It can be set up anywhere that a piece of fabric can be laid down and not be disturbed by children, other family members, household pets or visitors. It also needs to be somewhere you feel is appropriate and where you can arrange the altar with due ceremony; somewhere you will feel comfortable and have the privacy to meditate.

Why Meditate?

The purpose of meditation is to give yourself time and space away from the madding crowd, from the din and dullness of the world, from the pressure of everything that has to be done. It provides an opportunity for you to bloom, recharge your batteries, recuperate spiritually and become aware of your place in the universe. It gives you a break from your everyday life.

Meditating with the help of your goddess can be an alternative to taking a tea or coffee break, or watching the television. Meditation closes out the noise of what is immediately around you, gives you time and space to grow on your own, develop your spirituality, connect to the planet, rest and revive.

You probably already have in your life something you habitually do to centre yourself, to pull yourself together and to give yourself the strength to carry on. Making an altar and meditating with the goddess you have created combine to celebrate such an activity and make it a more significant part of your life. See pages 12–13 for an illustration of an altar containing several possible elements.

PHOTOGRAPH

This is a special personal item which celebrates an individual life.

METAL BELL

A bell to signify the start and end of your meditative time. You might choose a gong, a drum or a whistle.

WATER AND SEASHELL

A seashell comes from the ocean, the planet's watery depths. Placed in a bowl of fresh water it represents the element of water.

PINE CONE OR PIECE OF WOOD

These are examples from plant life of the continuous process of death and renewal.

STONE

This will put you in touch with the element of earth, the solid bedrock beneath our feet.

JEWELLERY

Use something with sentimental value, such as a family heirloom or a wedding ring. This represents the metal element.

CANDLE OR NIGHT LIGHT

Containing the elements of fire and
air, in a safe holder, these will
provide light and gentle
stimulation
for your eyes.

INCENSE

Secure burners into a piece of clay
– the earth element – or other
suitable holder. When ignited,
incense has the elements of fire
and air. Its aroma provides
soothing stimulation for the
sense of smell. Its curling smoke
is pleasing to behold.

GODDESS FIGURINE

Place your goddess in the
context of your own life
and the universal with
due ceremonial solemnity,
before beginning your
meditation.

13

FABRIC

This should be something you like and to which you have an emotional
attachment. This could vary from a piece which has been in your family
for a long time to an embroidered handkerchief.

The Elements of Your Altar

The illustration on the previous two pages shows an elaborate altar containing many different elements. You may choose to include some or all of these in your altar. Once you have chosen the place for your altar you should designate it as sacred by laying down a piece of fabric. This could be anything from a rich silk scarf to a favourite quilt, a piece of lace which has been in your family for a long time or a simple embroidered handkerchief. Any piece of fabric which is important to you is suitable. It can be draped over the edge of the table or shelf. Each of the items you choose to place on the altar is important for a different reason.

The fabric will provide something pleasant to touch with the palm of your hand or your fingertips, but you might like to add a feather for softness – or perhaps something prickly. You could also add something to tickle your taste buds such as a piece of chocolate. A bell, drum, gong or whistle will provide a clear sound to satisfy your sense of hearing, and can be used to mark the beginning and end of your meditation.

Representing the Planet

To connect your senses and your sense of yourself to the planet it helps to display elements of earth, air, fire and water on your altar. According to Chinese tradition, the elements of wood and metal are also included. Other elements may be important to you.

You can represent the planet with a favourite stone or pebble or piece of rock. A seashell is a reminder of the life-giving importance of the oceans and a bowl of fresh water represents the earth's rivers. Use a pine cone or a piece of wood showing the grain or the growth rings of a tree on your altar to represent the regeneration of nature.

Individuality

Having provided stimulation for your senses and items to show respect for the planet, add items which signify your individual life. These could be photographs of your loved ones, a piece of jewellery such as a ring or locket, even a pen or a postcard. Use anything which is special to you or to which you have an emotional attachment.

Beginning Your Meditation

Creating your own goddess may have taken you just an hour or a whole afternoon. Setting up your altar may also be a lengthy process. As you put it together, try to remember why you chose that particular figurine to create as your own goddess. Remember how you felt as you created her. What negative thoughts and emotions faded away during the creative process? What new, positive ones emerged? How will she inspire you and fire your creativity?

As you prepare to place your goddess on her altar, allow yourself to do so with due ceremony and when you are ready give yourself time to meditate. If your goddess has a guided meditation you may wish to record the words and listen to them whilst you sit in front of your altar. Alternatively, a friend could read the meditation to you. If your goddess has a meditative poem, hymn, prayer or piece of prose, you can read it to yourself silently or out loud as you contemplate its significance.

Make Time to Meditate

A full meditation, which may take up to an hour, needs to be scheduled in advance. At the appointed hour ignite your incense. Light your candle. Touch the fabric, the feather and other items on that altar. Feel the seashell, the stone, the wood, the water. Recall what your special items mean to you and give thanks for that meaning. Gaze at your goddess and give thanks for what she means to you. Ring your bell or strike your drum, breathe in deeply, breathe out slowly and enjoy fully your time of quiet contemplation.

If you have less time available, use the altar for a short meditation. Even ten minutes of focus and peace can have a beneficial effect on your life.

Silence and Time

You can meditate alone or with others, but the essential prerequisites are dedicated time and silence – or at least quietness. You might think of it as going off into a daydream. The silence is akin to the moment's silence often called for at a memorial service.

You can also meditate momentarily with a quick glance at a photograph of something or someone you love; perhaps a flower arrangement or a sleeping child.

Before You Begin...

Collect around you everything you may need to complete your model before starting. Try to create a calm, peaceful atmosphere, perhaps with some music. Work with the clay on a wooden or plastic chopping board. If you have an old one which you can use, so much the better. If not, the clay can be cleaned off the board after use with water with no ill-effects. Alternatively, work with the clay on the piece of plastic which it comes wrapped in. This also helpful to prevent your model sticking to the work surface, and makes it easier to move when you have finished.

To store an unfinished model overnight, dampen it and wrap in a plastic bag. Tie the bag shut with a rubber band, or twist the top to make it as air-tight as possible. Models stored in this way will keep for up to a week before the clay starts to dry out. A small clay model will only take a day or so to dry. Larger models may take up to three days to dry completely. The clay should be dry before varnishing or painting.

The modelling tool included in this kit will allow you to do most of the techniques required to make every model in this book. However, some of the models require other tools, most of which can be found around the home. These are shown below.

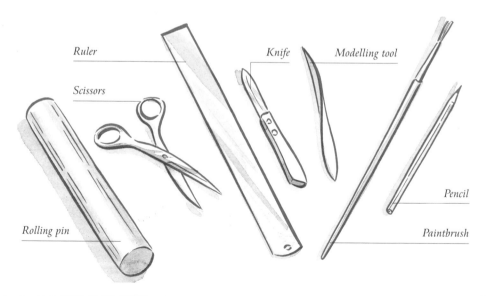

Ruler

Knife

Modelling tool

Scissors

Pencil

Rolling pin

Paintbrush

Modelling Techniques

$\textcircled{\textit{O}}$ver the following pages are the basic techniques that you will need to make all the models in this book, from the simplest to the most complicated. If you have worked with clay before you will already be familiar with many of these techniques. You may wish to read through this section quickly before starting your figurine, then refer back to it as you are making your goddess.

ROLLING OUT THE CLAY WITH A ROLLING PIN

ROLLING OUT A SAUSAGE OR CYLINDER

Set the rolling pin down on top of your square of clay. Starting on one side of the clay, press lightly down on your rolling pin. Roll backwards and forwards with light strokes until your clay reaches the desired size.

If you do not have a rolling pin, use a glass bottle or aerosol can or anything you may find around your home which is a smooth cylindrical shape.

Sometimes for a limb all you need is a small sausage of clay. Roll into a smooth sausage by pressing the piece of clay on to the tabletop and rolling it backwards and forwards with the palms of your hands. Smooth the outside with some water before adding it to your model.

To make a cylinder – the basic shape of many of the figures – simply use more clay and roll a thicker sausage.

PINCHING AND STRETCHING

To make a feature such as a nose or eye socket, pinch out a piece of clay with the thumb and index finger. Then continue adding other small pieces of clay to build up the surrounding area slightly.

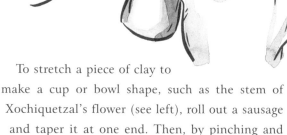

To make the base of a neck, pinch out from the top of a cylinder. Build up with small raisin-shaped pieces of clay

To stretch a piece of clay to make a cup or bowl shape, such as the stem of Xochiquetzal's flower (see left), roll out a sausage and taper it at one end. Then, by pinching and pulling gently, increase the length and form.

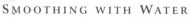

SMOOTHING WITH WATER

If the clay becomes too dry to work with, dip your fingertips into a bowl of water and transfer a little to the surface of the clay to smooth it down.

Also use water on your fingertips to stick extra pieces of clay such as arms and legs to a basic shape. This will create a tougher join.

Do not use too much water as the clay can easily become over-wet, and not good for modelling. If this happens, leave it uncovered and set it aside until it is the right consistency to model again.

THE 'SQUASHED-RAISIN' TECHNIQUE

This is a technique used to build up your figurine using small pieces of clay the size of a squashed raisin. It is used throughout the book to make limbs and to add detail.

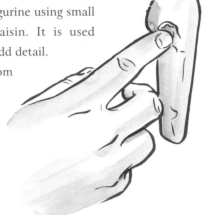

Break off raisin-sized pieces of clay from your main lump. Gently squeeze them and attach them to the area you need to build up – such as a shoulder – smoothing as you go. One raisin is smoothed on top of another to build up the clay gradually. Strengthen and fill in holes with more squashed raisins of clay.

JOINING TWO PIECES TOGETHER

19

Sometimes you will need to join an arm to a shoulder or a head to a neck. This can be done by placing the two pieces of clay to be joined next to each other and then pinching them together gently with your thumb, index and middle finger. You may then add a little water to smooth and strengthen the join. When you make a join of this kind it will often be very fragile to start with, so pinching it together and squeezing it in this way will strengthen it.

Making and Attaching a Head

1 Take a piece of clay which will be the correct size for the head of the model you are working on.

2 Roll the clay into an ovoid shape.

3 With your tool make a small hole in the base of the head. This will be used to join the head to the neck.

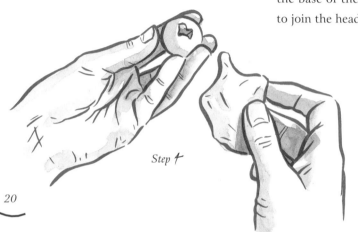

Step 1

4 Form the neck into a point where it has to join the head.

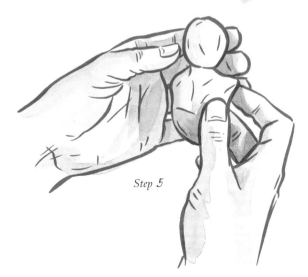

Step 5

5 Place the head onto the body.

6 Using the side of the modelling tool, smooth over the join between the head and neck.

7 If you want to strengthen the join, build up the back of the neck and shoulders with small raisins of clay to make a smooth connection.

MAKING A FACE

1 A face can be made simply by drawing on the eyes, nose, mouth and brows with a pencil.

This method is likely to be used when making the relief models such as Venus of Laussel, Inana and the Sacred Trio.

A more complex three-dimensional face can be made following steps 2 – 5 below.

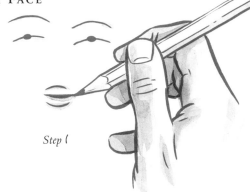

Step 1

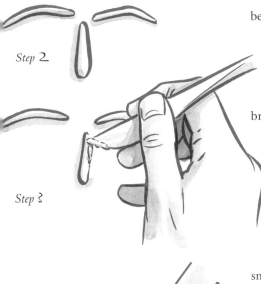

Step 2

Step 3

Step 5

2 To make a three-dimensional face, begin by rolling a small raisin of clay for the nose and position on the face. Make the eyebrows in the same way.

3 Make sure that the nose and brows are secure by pressing on them with your modelling tool. Wet the clay slightly if necessary and smooth down the edges, forming a strong join. Then shape the nose with the modelling tool.

4 Create the eyes by digging out small hollows and adding two small balls of clay into the centre of each hollow.

5 A raised mouth can be made by adding a small raisin and then adding shape to it with the modelling tool.

21

MAKING AND APPLYING HAIR

1 Roll out or shape the clay with your fingertips into the required shape for the hair. Make it too big, rather than too small, as you can trim it with your knife later.

2 Place it on top of your figurine's head and make sure that it is firmly stuck in place.

3 Smooth the hair into shape and, if you wish, add details of hair strands with your modelling tool.

22

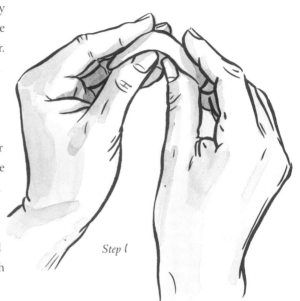

Step 1

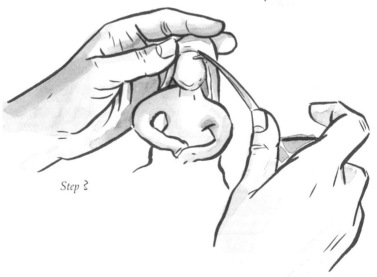

Step 3

Using the Modelling Tool

SKETCHING SHAPES OUT ON THE CLAY

This method is used on relief carvings to sketch out your image before carving or adding more detail. It may also be used to add detail to figurines such as Prajnaparamita (below). Take a pencil and draw the outline of the shape, pressing quite hard and scooping out bits of clay as you do this. Then use your modelling tool to go over and clarify the lines. For a more obvious shape, press the tool into the lines you have drawn and move it from side to side.

23

GOUGING OUT A SHAPE

This is a technique which can be used to give better definition to the legs in such figures as the Cycladic Grave Figurine or Isis. Using a pencil, draw the leg position then with your tool or knife, gouge out and cut away a small section of clay. Then squeeze the legs between thumb and forefinger to create greater definition in the thighs, calves and ankles.

SCRAPING AWAY CLAY TO FORM A RELIEF

When making one of the flat models you may need to scrape away from the edge of your drawing with the modelling tool or a knife. This will make the design stand proud from the flat background. Scrape downwards and outwards towards the edge of the relief. Do not remove too much clay, however, or the finished figurine will become weak.

STICKING A PIECE DOWN

This technique may be used to apply arms, legs, noses and anything else that is moulded separately from the main part of your figurine. If these more delicate pieces are not stuck down with care, they may fall off once your goddess is dry. Wet the piece slightly at one end and stick it into position.

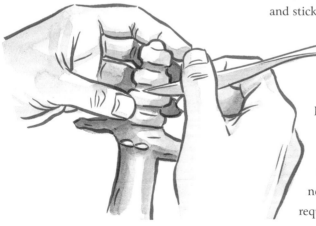

Press it down with your modelling tool, adding some small raisins of clay around the join to secure it, if necessary. Smooth it into the required shape.

THE

Goddesses

Venus of Laussel

FRANCE, 25,000 BCE

For: COSMIC CONNECTION

This voluptuous 'Venus', now named after the place where she was found, seems to represent the cycle of seasons and women's connection to it through their reproductive power. This cycle holds thirteen full moons and thirteen fertile moments for all women. From women flows the blood of life, and in their bellies babies grow. Women renew the community. From within them comes the future and they embody the cycle of seasons. Their bodies tell the time.

It is this sense of cosmic connection that is conveyed by the sacred Venus figurine, carved so long ago. She holds up a bison's horn with thirteen notches carved on it, pats her fertile belly, and speaks to all who see her. Some believe that her rounded belly shows that she is pregnant. She was probably revered and celebrated for her fertility and her beauty, as well as her connection with nature and the universe.

Ice-age Life

This Venus figure was carved into the rock face of a cave using tools made from hard stone or animal horn. Those who revered her lived in the ice age. This was the era of woolly mammoths and cave paintings.

Ice-age humans were forever on the move through the cold landscape in

This voluptuous figure was carved in the rock at the entrance to a cave in southern France in about 25,000 BCE. She can now be found in the Musée d'Aquitaine in Bordeaux, France.

family groups of twenty or thirty. They moved with nature's rhythms. They followed the seasons according to their inherited knowledge and wisdom. Their nomadic way of life sustained humanity for thirty thousand years. Most of the food for the group came from gathering roots, leaves, berries, fruits and nuts, from catching rabbits, hares and fish. If a dead animal was found, its meat was eaten and its pelt kept a baby warm.

At night the extended family regrouped to eat and sleep together. They sat around the campfire, which burned brightly inside a circle of stones. They might have meat from a successful hunt to eat with mushrooms, chestnuts and leaves for a salad. They had thawed ice and snow for drinking water. After the meal when they slept, the heat from the fire and each other's bodies kept them warm and alive.

Knowledge and Strength

Nomadic hunter-gatherers had a healthy lifestyle. They lived longer and suffered less sickness than their descendants, who settled down with flocks and farms. Among them as they moved – maybe even leading them – were many strong, knowledgeable women. They would mind the babies and children because their own offspring were now old enough to gather and hunt. They could answer questions and give advice. They remembered the routes of the migratory cycle, where and when nutritious plants appeared.

Finding food was not a full-time occupation. There was time to think, to feel, to teach, to have fun and be beautiful. There was time to spin and weave. The plants plucked from the ground for food had fibres in their stalks which could be woven into nets, baskets, bags and various textiles. Spinning and weaving were everyday work for the women. They combined these tasks with minding infants, teaching children and forming a focus for the family.

Celebrating the Cycle of Seasons

The passing of the seasons was also celebrated. People wore their best clothes and elaborately braided their hair to attend festivals to which many, many came from far and wide. They came to tell stories, to teach and learn, to find a mate. These festivals took place in special locations remembered and returned to at particular times in the cycle of seasons. Ancient people saw the connection between the cycles of women, the moon and plants.

28

MAKE YOUR ✳ ✳ ✳ Easy

Venus of Laussel

This figurine was carved in rock as a relief, which means that it is raised only slightly from the base rock. This can be recreated by moulding the figure directly from the clay in a tablet shape. Those who feel confident in clay work, however, might make this goddess as a three-dimensional figure. Whichever method you choose, concentrate particularly on building up the hips and legs of the figure and making her as rounded and voluptuous as possible. As it has particular significance the bison horn should also be a prominent feature.

YOU WILL NEED

- *Chopping board to work on*
- *Kitchen knife*
- *Rolling pin*
- *Ruler*
- *Pencil*
- *Modelling tool*
- *Water*

1 Cut a slice measuring about 1 cm (¼ in) and set to one side wrapped in plastic. This will be used later to build up the features of the figure.

2 Roll out the remaining clay to form a rectangular shaped tablet roughly 1 cm (½ in) thick, measuring about 12 cm by 10 cm (5 in by 4 in).

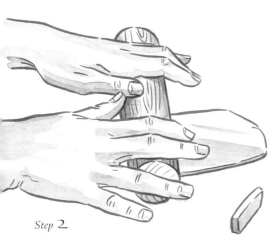

Step 2

3 Roughly sketch out the goddess figure on the clay using a pencil. Remember not to let the clay dry out too much.

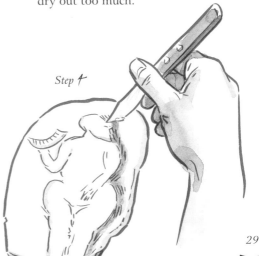

Step 3

29

4 Using a knife or the modelling tool, begin to carve away some of the clay from the outline of the figure, to create a raised piece which can be moulded into the Venus shape.

5 Using the clay which has been scraped away and the clay set aside from the original piece, begin to build up the figure of the Venus, using the picture of the original Venus on page 26 as your guide.

Concentrate especially on building up the shoulders and upper and lower arms using raisin-sized pieces of clay. The right arm is bent at 45 degrees up towards the head. Place a raisin of clay to create a cupped right hand.

8 Build up the left arm, making it rest on the tummy. Flatten a raisin of clay to create the left hand, smooth it down and mark out the five digits with a knife.

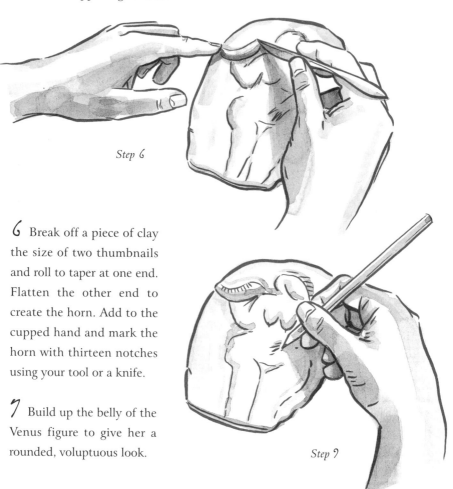

Step 6

6 Break off a piece of clay the size of two thumbnails and roll to taper at one end. Flatten the other end to create the horn. Add to the cupped hand and mark the horn with thirteen notches using your tool or a knife.

7 Build up the belly of the Venus figure to give her a rounded, voluptuous look.

Step 9

9 Draw out a pubic triangle with a pencil and indicate pubic hair. Perhaps indicate a slight depression in the clay of the tummy to mark the belly button. Hair could be indicated using a knife.

10 To finish, you could generally tidy up the figure with your modelling tool. Add the finishing touches by smoothing your figurine with fingers dipped into water.

Reflect on Your Venus of Laussel

Happy the person who discovers Wisdom,
the person who gains discernment:
gaining her is more rewarding than silver,
more profitable than gold.
She is beyond the price of pearls,
nothing you could covet is her equal.

In her right hand is length of days;
in her left hand, riches and honour.
Her ways are delightful ways,
her paths all lead to contentment.
She is a tree of life for those who hold her fast,
those who cling to her live happy lives.

Proverbs 3:13–18

Bird-headed Snake Goddess

EGYPT, 3500 BCE

For: ANCIENT FEMALE STRENGTH

This figurine links the earth to the sky in a sinuous snake-like upward movement. She has a long, elegant neck and abstract bird-like face. Her powerful arms lift and curve like cow horns. Strong and dignified, she is one of the world's oldest female images. Focus on her pose to stimulate your inner strength and well-being.

Before the Pharaohs

She was made in pre-dynastic Egypt long before the days of the Pharaohs and the pyramids. Whoever made her was descended from the people who lived around the lakes of the Sahara desert. These lakes expanded and shrank according to the amount of rainfall. While the men hunted gazelles and hares beyond the lakeside homesteads, the women took care of the domesticated cows. They often had to give them water from wells dug deep into the silt of lakes shrunken by drought.

The Cow Goddess

Egyptian religion originated in these harsh desert conditions, where water, cows, milk and women were the source of nourishment and regeneration. One of the earliest named Egyptian goddesses, the 'cow

This ancient figurine is now held in the Brooklyn Museum of Art, New York. She originated in Egypt.

goddess', Hathor, is sometimes shown with a woman's face and cow's ears. She was a cosmic, or celestial, cow who nourished the souls of the dead in heaven. Souls, imagined as birds, belonged to the sky. This may explain why this figurine – and many others like her – has raised arms resembling cow horns and also a bird face with a beak. She pre-dates the more famous Hathor and many of the other dynastic goddesses.

When the Egyptian cattle-herders were finally forced by drought to leave the desert, to settle on the banks of the River Nile and begin growing wheat and barley, they took their religious beliefs with them. Their cattle imagery was combined with the imagery of vegetation and the restorative power of the River Nile. Along with Hathor, the most prominent goddesses in Ancient Egypt – Neith, Nut and Isis – were all initially represented as cows. As mother goddesses they were fundamental to Egyptian religion, with its core notions of birth, death and resurrection.

Egyptian Burial Offerings

Religion and royalty became closely connected as Egyptian kingship was established along the River Nile. The religion was first recorded in the Pyramid Texts, dating from the fifth and sixth dynasties (2465–2250 BCE). Under the Pharaohs, Egyptian society became much more hierarchical, and the famous pyramids were built as tombs for the elite dead.

The Bird-headed Snake Goddess figurine was buried in an Egyptian grave one thousand years before the Pyramid Texts were written. At that time, graves of women were equal to, or larger than, those of men, with elaborate grave goods. This may have reflected their high status and their association with magical or religious powers, rooted in their nurturing associations.

With her raised arms and bird-like face, reminiscent of souls in the sky, she connects us directly to the Egyptian cow goddess Hathor. She seems to be dancing a ritual dance with a gesture still said to be used by women cattle herders in the Sudan, North Africa.

Now in New York, USA, she was excavated from a tomb at El Ma'mariya in Egypt by the French archaeologist Henri de Morgan in 1906. She is just under 30 cm high (1 ft) and is made of terracotta clay.

33

MAKE YOUR ✳ ✳ ✳ Moderate

Bird-headed Snake Goddess

The trick to making your bird-headed woman successfully is ensuring the strength and integrity of her slender neck, arms, thighs and bottom. These parts of her body need to be built up gradually using small, pinched-off pieces of clay around the size of a fingernail, and about the thickness of a squashed raisin.

YOU WILL NEED

- *Chopping board to work on*
- *Ruler*
- *Kitchen knife*
- *Modelling tool*
- *Water*

1 Roll the clay into a cylinder about 15 cm (6 in) long and 3 cm (1¼ in) thick. Make sure that there are no folds or air pockets in the clay and smooth it down with your fingers, so that there are no creases or dips.

2 With your modelling tool or a kitchen knife, cut off about one third of the clay cylinder and wrap it in plastic film to keep it damp and malleable. Put this piece aside to use later to make the head, arms, hips, thighs, bottom and breasts of your figurine.

3 Stand the remaining cylinder upright and make sure it has a flat base. About one-third from the top of the cylinder, mark the position of the waist with your modelling tool. Slightly squeeze the clay inwards at the waist, but do not yet make it as narrow as in the final statue.

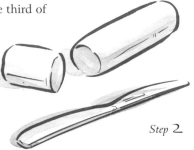

Step 2

4 Roll the cylinder so that it tapers from the waist to the base. Keep the base flat for the time being; it will be easier to work on while it can still stand up. While you work you may find it easier if you stick it to your board. Later, you may wish to taper her lower half to a peg-like point like the original, so that she can be stuck into sand or soil.

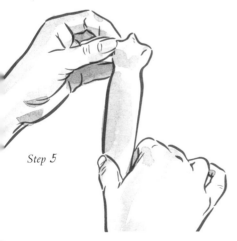

Step 4

5 Shape the top of the cylinder into three mounds, ready to attach the head and arms to. These form the base of the neck and the shoulders.

Step 5

6 Rotate the figurine slowly, meditating on which side is to be the front and which the back. Then, using the clay set aside in step 2, begin pulling out the arms.

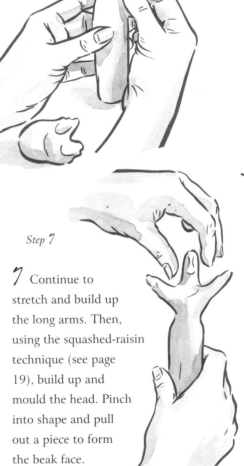

Step 6

35

Step 7

7 Continue to stretch and build up the long arms. Then, using the squashed-raisin technique (see page 19), build up and mould the head. Pinch into shape and pull out a piece to form the beak face.

8 When creating the arms, build up the back and across the shoulders as you go to add strength. Add clay to the arms using the squashed raisin technique, until they are about the width of a little finger. For a sense of stretch and movement, the arms need to lean backwards slightly. Dip your fingertips in water and stroke the clay of the arms to create solid, smooth lines. Finish off the hands above the head.

Step 10

Step 9

9 For the breasts make two small spheres, rolling them into elongated egg shapes, and mould them firmly on to the breast bone. Use the modelling tool to smooth the surface around and between the breasts.

10 Use more raisin-sized pieces of clay to build up the hips and thighs gradually. At the same time, narrow the waist until it is about the same width as the base, giving her a curvy hourglass figure.

11 Gently smooth over the surface of the figurine with a damp sponge.

12 Stroke downwards with a damp finger from the hips to suggest the separation of the legs. Or you could use your modelling tool to draw a faint vertical groove for a more definite line.

13 For extra detail, add another small piece of clay to her head for hair (but don't smooth it down), and score grooves for her fingers on the underside of her hands with the kitchen knife.

14 Using your kitchen knife, cut your figurine off the board. At this stage you might want to taper her legs further until they make a point like the original statuette. Carefully lie her flat to dry.

Reflect on Your Bird-headed Snake Goddess

My muse is in myself;
And as all past and future
Exist between my own two eyes,
My living need
Is symbolized
By her resplendent figure.

She stands behind the mountains
Like the sun,
And lifts her arms to show
That they are only flesh,
That all this valley is alive
Because she wills it so.

An extract from the poem Gloria *by Ruth Fainlight*

Inana

IRAQ, 3500 BCE

For: SEX AND POWER

Inana was the most important goddess in ancient Sumer; the birth-place of writing and the cradle of civilization. Inana was a goddess of war and sexual love and was known as the Queen of Heaven and Earth. She was young, beautiful and impulsive, and the many myths which survive about her show her strength and powerful sexuality.

The civilization that worshipped Inana was at its height in the fourth and third millennia BCE in ancient Sumer, known to the Greeks as Mesopotamia, and now Iraq. It was here that the world's first literature was produced, written on clay tablets in two languages, Sumerian and Akkadian. In the Akkadian language Inana was known as Ishtar, and that name lives on as a major topographical feature on Venus.

Queen of Heaven and Earth

The power and authority of this ancient goddess can still be felt today. If you choose to make your own Inana, you

This is an image made by rolling a cylinder seal across wet clay. The cylinder seal was carved in Iraq in about 3500 BCE. It is now in the National Museum in Baghdad, Iraq.

will be celebrating and feeling her power all over again. As you read just a few of the myths about her, this power will become apparent.

The Many Faces of Inana

For more than three thousand years, this great goddess Inana had a starring role in the mythology and poetry of Sumerian and Akkadian literature. She has many aspects and is a complex figure who has many different characteristics manifested in the numerous myths surrounding her.

Her power, however, is never disputed. It is revealed in the myth which describes how she went to the home of the God of Ingenuity in the watery depths of Eridu, the oldest city in Sumer, where the writings of divine authority were kept. After drinking beer together, he handed over the writings to her and she set off in the boat of heaven to take them to her city, Unug.

When the God of Ingenuity sobered up and realized what he had done he sent his attendant in hot pursuit. Inana responded by sending him back with an earth-shattering cry, and the writings of divine authority were kept in Unug amidst much rejoicing.

Punishing Shu-kale-tuda

One day, whilst returning to Unug after time spent in the mountains, Inana rested in the shade of a tree with the writings of divine authority in her lap. While she slept a gardener's boy, Shu-kale-tuda, raped her, violating the writings of divine authority. When she awoke and discovered what had happened the angry Inana punished the land of Sumer three times. Shu-kale-tuda confessed to his father but escaped capture by hiding with his brothers in the city. Eventually, the God of Ingenuity, caught and humbled him.

'You must die,' Inana told Shu-kale-tuda, 'but your name will live on in song from the glorious royal palace to the lowliest shepherd's hut.'

Inana in the Underworld

The best-known Inana myth tells of her descent to the underworld ruled by her sister, Ereshkigal. Passing through the seven gates, she arrived divested of the symbols of her divine authority and was turned into a piece of rotting meat hanging from a hook on the wall. The God of Ingenuity intervened to save her but she had to choose a substitute to take her place in the underworld.

39

Her husband, the shepherd-god Dumuzi, had been given a new flute and coat on the orders of Ereshkigal. When Inana found him, he was not mourning her but entertaining young women.

'Take him!' she cried.

Drawing on Inana's Power

Inana's courtship and wedding with Dumuzi were recreated annually in Sumer with the sacred marriage rite. During this the king made love to a priestess representing Inana. By doing this he renewed his power, legitimized his rule and ensured economic prosperity for his people.

Consider the many people who have worshipped her in the past and feel your connection to their lives and imaginations. Read again her stories and remember Inana, Queen of Heaven and Earth.

MAKE YOUR   ✳ ✳ ✳ Easy
Inana

This image of Inana is an impression made on to a clay tablet by rolling across it a cylinder seal carved in white limestone. It shows Inana gazing protectively over her temple in the city of Unug. The eight-petalled rosettes and gate-posts like shepherds' crooks are Inana's symbols. The impression of the cylinder on the clay is recreated when making the model, and some of the details are built up using small sausages of clay. The rest of the image can be drawn with pencil. Focus on the wide eyes and facial expression of Inana.

YOU WILL NEED

- *Chopping board to work on*
- *Kitchen knife*
- *Rolling pin*
- *Ruler*
- *Plastic bottle or lid*
- *Pencil*
- *Modelling tool*
- *Water*

1 Cut a slice about 5 mm (¼ in) thick from your piece of clay and set aside wrapped in plastic. This will be used to build up the detail later.

2 Roll the rest of the clay out flat with a rolling pin into the shape of a long rectangular tablet, roughly 20 cm (8 in) long and 9 cm (3½ in) wide and 5 mm (¼ in) in thickness. Cut off any excess with your knife. These measurements do not have to be followed precisely; roll the clay out to a thickness you are happy with.

used to make the original tablet, roll it across the middle of the tablet, pressing hard. Keep rolling until you have created an impression in the centre of the tablet and the edges are thicker than the centre.

Step 4

Step 3

3 Find a suitable object (a small plastic bottle, for example), which is slightly narrower than the width of your tablet. To create the impression of the cylinder

4 Next, using a pencil or your modelling tool, sketch out the image roughly on to the tablet. Use the original on page 38 as your guide to include the face of Inana, the stars (eight-petalled rosettes) which are her symbols next to her, the long outline of her chin and the temple on the right. If you are not happy with your design smooth it over and start again.

5 Take up the clay set aside in step 1. Break it into two equal pieces and roll one of them into a long thin sausage to use as Inana's chin and arched boundary line. Make the sausage as thin as you can – about 5 mm – (¼ in) in diameter and slightly longer than it needs to be so that it can be moulded into shape.

Step 6

42

6 Place the long sausage on top of your sketched line for the long arch and press down to make sure it is fixed in position. Smooth down the edges of the sausage to make a join with the tablet.

8 Take the remaining piece of clay and break off a piece to make the nose. Mould into a small lozenge shape and press into position on Inana's face. Ensure it is firmly stuck by wetting the clay if necessary and smoothing down the edges with your modelling tool.

9 Take two small pieces of clay from the piece you have left and roll into two equally-sized balls. Place them in the middle of each drawn oval-shape to create the eyes.

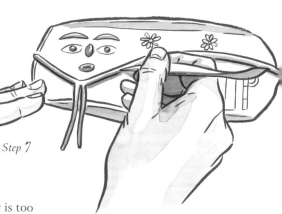

Step 7

7 Use the edge of your modelling tool to give the top of the line a sharper ridge. If the clay is too dry, smooth down with a little water.

(0 To create the eyebrows roll two small sausages and position, again pressing down with the modelling tool. If you feel confident, you may use progressively smaller pieces of clay to go over your outline of the eyes, lips, gate-posts and stars. However, if this proves too fiddly, then strengthen your original drawing with a sharp pencil.

Reflect on Your Inana

From the midst of heaven my lady
  looks down with joy,
Her grandeur expanding to heaven's
  edge.
I praise the young lady, Inana.

The black-headed people parade for her
  joyfully,
Filling the palace, her platform is ready,
The king awaits Inana.

In the New Year rites she decides our
  destiny.
As the moon disappears she perfects her
  powers.
Her bed is made, Inana.

She bathes her holy thighs, she
  sprinkles fragrant oil.
In Inana's holy thighs the king rejoices
  proudly.
'My beloved,' says Inana.

Hymn to Inana

43

Sleeping Lady of Malta

MALTA, 3000 BCE

For: REST, RECUPERATION AND RECOVERY

On the island of Malta was found this tiny clay goddess-like figure known as the 'Sleeping Lady of Malta'. She was found in a huge underground burial chamber. Small enough to hold in the palm of the hand, she has the gravitas of the monumental figures found above ground. Placed among those who had died, she exudes softness and warmth as she reclines, so restful and tranquil. She remains a mysterious figure. Is she laid low by the pain of menstruation?

This clay figurine was made in Malta in about 3000 BCE and placed in a burial chamber. She is now in the National Museum in Malta.

Is she recovering from childbirth? Has she suffered a miscarriage? Is she recuperating from illness? Perhaps she absorbed the pains of her people, their trials and tribulations? Maybe she is dreaming for them, or waiting for the answers to questions come to her. As she naps on her couch she is so ancient yet so modern. She is strange and yet familiar. She is so different and yet, to this day, so very easy to identify with.

Goddess Worship in Malta

Malta, which lies to the south of Italy, is less than thirteen miles long and nowadays is very densely populated. It is still venerated as a site of goddess worship. The ancient stone buildings on the island are the work of people whose history and way of life remain so mysterious they are known simply as 'the temple builders'. They journeyed from Sicily seven thousand years ago, bringing cattle, sheep, and seeds for wheat and barley. Malta was then inhabited by red deer and bears. The island had few natural resources apart from farmland, clay and limestone rock.

In this demanding and isolated place the ancient Maltese established a society which lasted more than five thousand years. They left no evidence of warfare or weapons. They had no metal for tools, but used flint, deer horns and stone axes. With these tools they built the temples from the limestone rock for which they are famous.

Temples of the Goddess

The temples are huge and curvaceous. From the air each temple is the shape of a voluptuous woman or mother-goddess, as are the carved figures installed within them. The stone slabs used to build the temples were moved, not on cylindrical rollers, but on large spherical stones. On cylindrical rollers a heavy slab can be moved only in straight lines. On spherical stones it can be moved in any direction, as if on ball-bearings.

The temples were used as sacred places dedicated to religious activity for more than two thousand years. Special rites were performed in a screened-off area. The inside walls were smoothed and painted with red ochre. There were decorative carvings of plants, animals and spirals.

The Cycle of Life

In about 3000 BCE, work began at Hal Saflieni on a mass burial chamber – a

45

hypogeum – beneath the temple. Two thousand tons of limestone rock were chiselled out. The *hypogeum* mirrors the temple above it and took a thousand years to build. It was built to be the last resting place for six thousand bodies.

The *hypogeum* was decorated with red ochre spirals. Here the people of ancient Malta returned to the embrace of the earth which had given birth to them and nurtured them while they lived. A niche carved in the chamber known as 'the oracle room' enhances the deep natural echo. In here, sound reverberates as a comforting reminder of the endless cycle of birth, life and death. The resonance makes a soothing music, a calming balm. It is the perfect place for dream incubation and a fitting place for the sleeping lady to be found.

MAKE YOUR ✳ ✳ ✳ Moderate

Sleeping Lady of Malta

This figure is moulded from one piece of clay, apart from the bed on which she lies. This means that making her involves moulding, rather than building up the figure and adding separate pieces to her. Follow the original figure and make your sleeping lady with wide hips and an ample bosom. Also, try to convey the sense of peace and rest in her face and her pose; the feeling you get from the original Maltese figure.

YOU WILL NEED

- *Chopping board to work on*
- *Kitchen knife*
- *Rolling pin*
- *Ruler*
- *Modelling tool*
- *Pencil*
- *Water*

1 From your piece of clay cut off a 2 cm (¾ in) slice to make the base of the sleeping figure's bed. Set the remainder aside for a few minutes, wrapped in plastic to keep it damp enough to work with later.

2 Press, or roll, the small piece into an oblong bed-shape, which should be about 5 mm (¼ in) thick. If necessary, round off the corners of the bed with a knife and smooth down with some water.

3 Take the large lump of clay discarded in step 1. Cut off two small pieces and roll them into sausages for the bed supports.

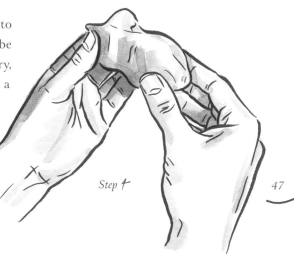

Step 3

Attach them to the base of the bed, making sure they are stuck securely by adding water and smoothing with the modelling tool if necessary. Set the bed aside while you work on the body of your figure.

Step 4

47

4 Take the large piece of clay and cut off a slice measuring 1½ cm (¾ in). Set to one side (this will be used to build up the figure, make a pillow, her hair and breasts). The piece you now have left is to be moulded into the head, body and arms of your sleeping figure. Start by making a rounded cylindrical shape which is roughly the length of the bed. Rough out the position of the head, shoulders, waist and feet.

5 Pinch the waist in further and add raisins of clay (see page 19) from the slice you cut off to build up substantial upper arms. For the lower arms, elbows and hands use larger squashed raisins, and smooth down. Continue adding shape with your modelling tool.

rough patches or concave surfaces. The figure should be as rounded and voluptuous as possible.

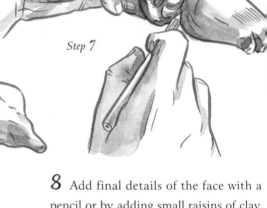

Step 7

Step 5

6 Add two small balls of clay for her breasts and build up the large hips and bottom with more raisins.

7 Smooth down the body and clothing using the modelling tool, and draw in the skirt hem and patterns on her clothes. Add hair (see page 22) and work on all sides of the figure to fill her out and make sure there are no holes,

8 Add final details of the face with a pencil or by adding small raisins of clay. If you prefer, leave her face blank to allow for deeper contemplation when meditating.

9 Take the remainder of the clay to make a small pillow for the head. Attach the completed figure to the bed with her head resting on the pillow.

Reflect on Your Sleeping Lady of Malta

... Imperceptible movement,
   only a
wave of glory, glorious deep
purple, thick, bruisy, tulip bloom,
followed by full crimson finally
plopping, wet poppy leaf dropping
to gleam a glass ruby, vermilion
yet to come, reminiscent of
   girlhood.

And now the jug pours portions
   of port wine
Rusting within, wounded, ripped,
Torn off a strip

The bandages
Absorb, commemorate, record
Marks of the mighty deluge ...

What's the secret?

All the nether region glistens with
   ache,
Daubed, dented, bricks missing,
Inflamed, engorged, even
   estranged.

Tiamat's* blood spurts through me
Splattered by the mighty god
   Marduk*.
After so many outbursts of
   bleeding
It's again surprising how it feels,
How forgotten it always is
Until the myth's reopened ...

Hurt fades
And there's nothing like it
Till next time.

Fran Hazelton

* *Characters from the Babylonian myth of creation.*

Cycladic Grave Figure

CYCLADIC ISLANDS, 2500 BCE

For: TRANQUILLITY

This ancient sacred female form carved from white marble has a strikingly modern appearance. The sculptor skilfully rubbed her with a special abrasive to achieve a polished finish. Her beautiful luminosity brings her face to life. She has no formal eyes or mouth and yet we almost see them. She seems to be staring inscrutably into the future.

She is one of many such distinctive figures found in 1883 and 1884 in the two hundred Cycladic islands which lie in the Aegean sea between the island of Crete and mainland Greece. They were looted from their original find spot and have been described as 'orphaned'. This carved figure was plucked from her geographical, social and historical context. She was lifted out of time as well as out of the earth, and is strangely disembodied.

The appeal of making such a figure today lies in the peaceful feeling she conveys to those who look upon her. With her expressionless face and her plain and beautiful form, meditate on her for peace in your life.

This polished marble figurine is one of many in this style carved in the Cycladic Islands close to Greece in about 2500 BCE. She is now in the National Museum of Cycladic and Ancient Greek Art, Athens, Greece.

Personification of the Earth

In this she is like artistic expressions of Gaia, the Greek goddess usually depicted as a woman emerging breast-high from the Earth itself. Gaia is the living presence of the Earth. She is a reminder of the time when matter was still rebellious, long before it could be perceived as *terra firma*.

Gaia signifies all that cannot be brought under control. She is eruptive and alive. She is Earth made invisible, Earth become metaphor, Earth as the realm of the soul. She is for life but for ever-renewing, ever-changing life, for life as it encompasses death. She is the divine Earth, the mother of men and of the gods who nourishes all, gives all, brings all to fruition and destroys all.

A Meditative Face

This Cycladic carving was originally found in a grave lying down, but as a standing figure she is an image of unbowed femininity. Her arms are folded. Her shoulders are firm. Her breasts, like her facial features, are barely indicated. Her large head on a strong neck is a backward, sweeping wedge shape with a streamlined, beak-like nose.

Some say this gives her a vulture-like look. Vultures were thought to be female and were worshipped as symbols of the female principle. Others say that her face is empty, yet so full of meaning, because she is in a trance-like state. She is an artist's impression of the death of the ego that is necessary for deep meditation.

Purpose of the Figurines

Most of the Cycladic figurines, like this one, were found in graves among the remains of the dead, and not on settlement sites. Sometimes two or more were found in a grave. The figurines are mostly female and some look pregnant. The one in twenty who are male are shown hunting or playing a musical instrument, such as the pipe or harp. There are also some animals.

Over the years, there have been many suggestions from scholars as to how these figurines functioned in the society which created them, and which lived in peace for nearly a thousand years. They may have been designed to satisfy the sexual appetite of the deceased. They may have been substitutes for human sacrifice. They may have been images of venerated ancestors. They may have been toys to amuse the dead. They may represent a guardian angel or spirit companion who would care for the person who had died, on their journey to the underworld.

Standing the Test of Time

One thing is for sure; the art of female spirituality in this Cycladic grave figure has stood the test of time. Her aesthetic appeal is undimmed over the four thousand years after she was first carved from local marble and polished to perfection. She remains a mysterious figure. Whatever she meant to those who then lived on the Cycladic islands, she is now an icon of quiet self-containment and calm.

MAKE YOUR ✳ ✳ ✳ Moderate

Cycladic Grave Figure

When making this model take special care with the proportions of the body. Notice she does not have exaggerated hips, breasts and thighs like many of the other figurines in this book, and that her legs are quite strong and muscular. Also, her head is large in proportion with her body, is square in shape and sits on a relatively thick neck. As these figures were found lying in graves, it does not matter if your figure does not stand up. You may find it soothing to hold her in your hand while you meditate or you may prefer to lay her down on your altar.

YOU WILL NEED

- *Chopping board to work on*
- *Kitchen knife*
- *Ruler*
- *Modelling tool*
- *Pencil*
- *Water*

1 Cut a small piece off the shorter side of your rectangle of clay (a slice about 1 cm/½ in wide). Roll the remaining piece into a cylinder which stands about 12 cm (5 in) high.

4 Roll two small balls for the breasts from the leftover clay. Attach these to the body and use your modelling tool to shape them and smooth them down.

Step 2

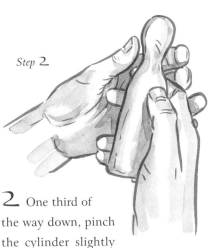

2 One third of the way down, pinch the cylinder slightly to create the wide neck of the figurine and to form the head. Continue to pinch lightly all the way round, turning the cylinder in your hands as you do so. Mark the position of the nose with your knife.

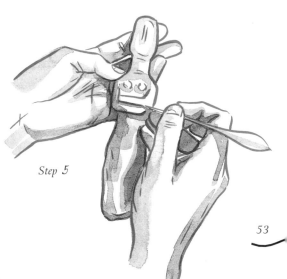

Step 5

53

Step 3

3 Begin shaping the torso, drawing out the shoulders and tops of the arms. Build up the shoulders and arms and elbows, using some of the clay from step 1.

5 Draw on the arms folded at the front of the body with a pencil.

6 Build up the head using small raisins, especially around the chin and sides of the face. It should be quite large and square in shape.

7 The distance from the head to the waist should be half, or slightly more than half, the height of the figure. Mark the waist by drawing a line on the clay.

Step 8

8 Next, cut out a groove between the legs below where you marked the waist. Work out the position of your figurine's knees, ankles, heels and toes. Then squeeze and build each up with small pieces of clay. Use the picture of the original Cycladic figure to help you create the right shape.

54

Step 9

9 Now flatten and smooth your figure to achieve its final marble-like finish with water on your fingertips. You may also wish to smooth down the front and back of your figure to flatten her in the Cycladic style.

Reflect on Your Cycladic Grave Figure

After you have created your own Cycladic Grave Figure and she is dry, set aside at least fifteen minutes when you can be in silence and won't be disturbed. Hold her in the palm of your hand and contemplate her shape. Run your hands over the clay.

How does it feel? Is it smooth? Wet? Warm? Cool? Look at her perfect simplicity. There are no fussy details. Only a nose to breathe appears on her serene face. No hair and no other facial details break up her smooth form.

Lie down on your back or sit comfortably, close your eyes and keep stroking the smooth clay. Place your hand on your forehead and relax your face. Smooth away any furrows in your forehead. Acknowledge your own cares and worries, then set them aside for ten minutes. Let them go. Begin your time of silence.

Take deep breaths in and out relaxing each part of your body as you do so. Flex your neck slightly then let the tension go. Relax your shoulders, chest, solar plexus, stomach and buttocks. Go from head to toe, wriggling then relaxing each part.

When you have been through each area of tension in your body, pause to take in the gift of profound peace that comes from this figure. Breathe it deep inside yourself and hold it there. Breathe out any remaining tension. Breathe in the gift of tranquillity, hold it inside on the in-breath. Discover the sense of deep repose.

When you return your attention to the room you are in, write down any words or memories which came to you in this time of silence, or draw a picture of anything which you received.

Sheena Barnes

55

Isis

EGYPT, 500 BCE

FOR: CONSTANCY

Isis was the greatest goddess of ancient Egypt. People believed in her, worshipped her and felt protected by her outstretched wings for nearly four thousand years. She was the mistress of magic and the speaker of spells. She was the divine mother. Read some of the many mythical stories written about her and use her power to bring constancy and strength into your life.

Isis and Osiris

Isis was the child of the sky-god and the earth-goddess. So, too, was Osiris, the mythical first king of Egypt and creator of civilization. Isis and Osiris loved each other even in the darkness of their mother's womb, but their brother Seth was envious. He tricked Osiris into climbing into a large chest which was sealed and flung into the River Nile.

Revival of Osiris

Isis searched far and wide for Osiris and finally found him in a foreign land. When his body was put in a boat bound for Egypt, Isis

The goddess Isis is shown here with her son, Horus, in a statuette made of bronze, encrusted with gold, which dates from the Egyptian late period. It is now held in the Louvre Museum, in Paris, France.

56

hovered lovingly above him, bringing him momentarily back to life. It was then that their son Horus (the child often depicted on the knees of Isis) was conceived.

While Isis cared for Horus, Seth found Osiris' hidden body as he hunted for wild boar in the moonlight. He ripped it to pieces and scattered the pieces. With the help of other gods Isis found all the pieces, except the penis, which had been swallowed by a fish. She made a replica and Osiris was put together again as a mummy.

Isis fanned the mummy with her wings and Osiris revived to become the ruler of eternity, who sits in the underworld judging the souls of the dead. Isis then protected Horus until he had grown old enough to take his father's place and avenge his death.

Goddess of Moon and Sea

Isis had many roles in Egyptian society. She was one of the deities connected with death rites. The sacred blood of Isis and its properties of protection and revitalization were symbolized in the girdle, or knot, of Isis, which was laid on mummified bodies. Made of red material, it resembled the vulva or womb of the goddess, and suggested regenerative powers.

Isis was also linked by the Egyptians with the dog-star Sirius, which rose at the inundation of the Nile and was therefore a symbol of abundance and the renewal of life. And she was linked with the moon and the sea, as protectress of navigators, like the Virgin Mary, with the Stella Maris – the 'star of the sea'. She was also 'Green Isis', the personification of cornfields, and lady of bread and beer, often shown with corn on her headdress.

The relationship between Isis and her son, Horus, was believed to be the ideal. She was one of the most important mother goddesses and a goddess of protection for her role in the guardianship of her son.

Spread of the Cult of Isis

Classical accounts indicate the worship of Isis by the Greeks and Romans, who were immensely influenced by her cult and worshipped her alongside their own gods. The fullest account of this can be found in *The Golden Ass* by Apuleius, a Roman who was initiated into the mysteries of the cult of Isis in the second century CE.

MAKE YOUR ✳ ✳ ✳ Challenging

Isis

Isis is one of the more complicated figures to make, although she is impressive when completed as she has beautiful detailing and a great horned headdress. As you can see from the examples on page 60–61, she is made without the seat which the original sat on, and can therefore sit on the edge of a table or shelf when you erect your altar. If, however, you have some extra clay and would prefer, you can, of course, make her with the block to sit on.

YOU WILL NEED

- *Chopping board to work on*
- *Modelling tool*
- *Pencil*

- *Water*
- *Knife*
- *Ruler*

1 Cut the clay in half and roll one half into a cylinder roughly 15 cm (6 in) long. Store the other piece in plastic to use later, for the head and other details.

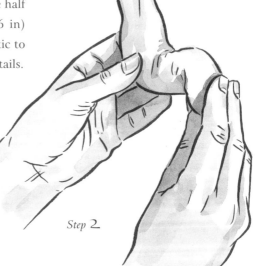

2 Bend the cylinder in the middle to make a seated figure, then bend back the lower part in half again, to form the knees and make the seated shape of Isis.

   Place your figure on the edge of a small box or other square object while you work on her.

Step 2

3 Form the legs by cutting away some clay from the bottom of the seated figure. Squeeze to taper the legs, then pinch to define the knees.

Step 6

Step 3

4 Bend the ends of the tapered legs out at right angles to create the feet of your Isis.

5 Pull out the shoulders from your main piece of clay. Squeeze a neck and the start of the arms, by pressing the clay between the thumb, index and middle fingers.

6 Roll a ball for the head using a piece of clay set aside earlier. Make a hole at the bottom and attach it to the

pointed neck (see page 20). Smooth down the join with your modelling tool, adding raisins of clay to strengthen, if necessary.

7 Use raisins of clay from the piece set aside in step 1 to build up the arms, bending them at the elbows. Pinch two hands on to the wrists.

8 Next, add the hair using the technique outlined on page 22. Use the picture of the original Isis to guide you. Smooth the hair down with some water.

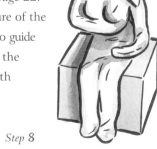

Step 8

Step 9

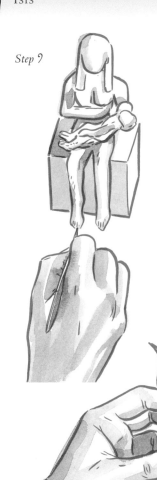

9 Make Horus (the baby) as a smaller version of Isis, starting with a cylinder, then bending it into shape before adding detail.

Position Horus on Isis's lap with her left arm supporting his head. Her right hand should be moulded to hold her left breast.

10 To form Isis's horns, roll a thin sausage about 10 cm (4 in) long and cut it in half. Roll a small ball and flatten on one side to form the sun, then mould the horns around it, making sure that they are secured to the sun-shape.

11 Stick the horns and sun on to Isis's head, strengthening the join and securing them with some small raisins of clay. Finish making the headdress by drawing on the serpent's head decoration and, if you wish, add the small bird's head at the front.

Step 11

12 Roll out a small rectangle of clay to make the skirt and smooth over the legs of the seated figure.

13 Mould the face (see page 21) and attach small pieces of clay for the ears. Draw on any final details including the necklace.

Step 12

Reflect on Your Isis

'I am Nature, the Universal Mother, mistress of all the elements, primordial child of time, sovereign of all things spiritual, queen of the dead, queen also of the immortals, the single manifestation of all gods and goddesses that are. My nod governs the shining heights of heaven, the wholesome sea breezes, the lamentable silences of the world below. Though I am worshipped in many aspects, known by countless names and propitiated with all manner of different rites, yet the whole round earth venerates me.'

Apuleius

Goddess of Growth

INDIA, 100 CE

For: RENEWAL

This beautiful goddess symbolizes the renewal of the earth's fertility. She comes from India, where such goddesses have been worshipped for more than five thousand years. Think of her if you need to make a fresh start in your life.

Ritual purification was important for goddess worship in India, as water is needed for crops to grow, which in turn nourish and sustain people. In the same way, the great mother goddess is closely connected with growth and renewal. For this reason many of the houses in ancient cities were equipped with elaborate drainage systems. To symbolize the female as the carrier of life, sacred pots were made. On these pots, a nude female figure was often depicted upside-down with her legs apart and vegetation issuing from her yoni (genitalia). Similar pots are still made and used today.

Shakti

Female symbols of plenty, purifying rivers and sacred trees have all become lasting features of the art of spirituality in India. Today, millions of Hindus worship the goddess in various forms. Her

This charming figurine was made in India in about 100 CE. She is now in the Museum of Asiatic Arts in Paris, France.

power is called 'Shakti' and is linked with the kundalini energy latent in the base of the spine.

Shakti texts written down in about 200 CE have been preserved as tantras. In the yoni tantra menstrual blood is 'the flower'. The feminine creative principle is 'the world from her womb'. Shakti is spontaneous vibration. The whole universe is a manifestation of Shakti. When Shakti expands or opens the universe comes into being. When Shakti gathers in or closes the universe disappears. In an endless cycle of opening and closing Shakti brings into existence countless universes.

Independence and Substance

The goddess alternates between eternal manifestation and dissolution. In dissolution she absorbs the cosmos of physical objects and everything collapses into the 'bindu', or seed-state. She is known as 'independence' or 'freedom' because her existence does not depend on anything apart from herself. She is known as 'substance' because all possible objects are latent and manifest in her womb.

Every female is a manifestation of Shakti. Female power revolves around life maintaining. It is not a power over others, but the power of life. A woman's power of life comes from her control of cooking and food distribution in the household. This is a variant of her power to give life and nourishment to the unborn child and the infant.

In the famous Hindu epic, *The Mahabharata*, a princess called Draupadi is lost in a game of dice played by her husband. She is dragged by her long flowing hair into the men's hall and the man who won her orders her to be disrobed. By divine intervention her garment becomes endless, and the more it is pulled, the more it renews itself. Draupadi's garment symbolizes the earth's vegetation and she represents the earth and the power of regeneration.

Death and Rebirth

Regeneration is an endless cycle of birth, growth, maturation, decay and death. For Hindus, death is like a sleep inside the mother's womb. It is a necessary transition before rebirth and regeneration. The regenerative power of women is the power they have over life and death.

Female sexuality is associated with the power to bring on fertilizing rain and the growth of vegetation. Sacred figurines often emphasize the yoni and have an abundance of hair or a floral headdress. On many statues, the yoni has been touched by generations of worshippers as a source of fertility.

Nature and goddess worship have been associated since ancient times. The Ganges river is an especially sacred and powerful female force. The waters flowing from the Himalaya mountains are believed to be extraordinarily purifying and millions of pilgrims wash away their sins by bathing in 'Mother Ganga'. Use the Goddess of Growth to make a fresh start in your life.

MAKE YOUR

Goddess of Growth

64

When making this goddess, keep details as simple as possible. The flowers in her hair should be bold and large, as should her earrings. When shaping the face, keep it fairly flat and large to accommodate her exaggerated facial features.

YOU WILL NEED
- *Chopping board to work on*
- *Kitchen knife*
- *Rolling pin*
- *Modelling tool*
- *Pencil*
- *Water*

1 Cut off one-third from your piece of clay and set aside. Roll the remainder into a sausage about 18 cm (7 in) long.

2 As you roll the sausage, press slightly harder on one side to form tapered legs.

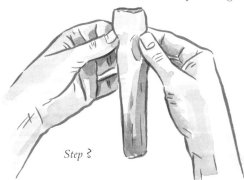

Step 2

3 One quarter of the way down the figure, start to pinch the head (see page 20). As you do this the triangular shoulders will start to emerge. Draw these out to form the short arms.

4 Underneath the shoulders and arms, less than halfway down your figure, start to pinch the waist into shape. As you pinch, continue to shape the head, neck, shoulders and the beginnings of the arms, and flatten the belly and legs slightly.

Step 5

5 Take up your rolling pin and roll gently downwards from the waist, across the tummy down to the tapered feet so that the front of the figurine is flat rather than rounded.

6 Take up the clay set aside in step 1. Break off six squashed raisins to build up the front of the head. Add two more raisins (rolled into sausages) and stick them to either side of the head from the middle of the forehead, tapering towards the chin, to create the hair. Draw on her hair detail with a pencil.

Step 6

7 Break off five more raisins the size of a thumbnail. Roll them into balls, then roll or press out flat to create the basic flower shape and the earrings.

8 Break off six smaller pieces of clay about 1 cm (½ in) across – these will make the eyes, necklace and the centre of the flowers. Roll into balls and place three of them into the centres of three of the larger discs to create the flowers. Use your knife to mark out the flower petals.

65

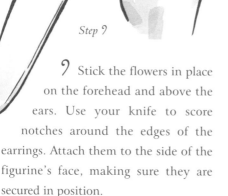

Step 9

9 Stick the flowers in place on the forehead and above the ears. Use your knife to score notches around the edges of the earrings. Attach them to the side of the figurine's face, making sure they are secured in position.

10 Roll out a long sausage of clay for the necklace and wrap it twice round the goddess's neck. Smooth down and make sure it is fixed securely. Score markings on the necklace with a knife.

11 Take another raisin from your remaining lump and roll it into a ball. Flatten it, and add three notches with a knife or your modelling tool, then add to the necklace as the central pendant.

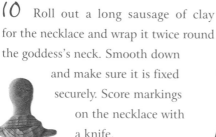

Step 13

12 Finally, add two little balls of clay on either side of the pendant to form the breasts. Smooth them down with a little water.

13 Use your knife or modelling tool to draw on the legs, the leg-bangles and girdle.

Reflect on Your Goddess of Growth

Woman is the creator of the
  universe,
The universe is her form.
Woman is the foundation of the
  world,
She is the true form of the body.
Whatever form she takes,
Whether the form of a man or a
  woman
Is the superior form.
In woman is the form of all things,
Of all that lives and moves in the
  world.
There is no jewel rarer than a
  woman,
No condition superior to that of a
  woman.
There is not, nor has been
  nor will be

Any destiny to equal that of a
  woman;
There is no kingdom, no wealth,
To be compared with a woman;
There is not, nor has been,
  nor will be
Any holy place like unto a woman.
There is no prayer to equal a
  woman.
There is not, nor has been,
  nor shall be
Any yoga to compare with a
  woman,
No mystical formula nor ascetism
To match a woman
There are not, nor have been,
  nor will be
Any riches more valuable than a
  woman.

Tantric hymn to Shakti

67

Sacred Trio

ENGLAND, 300 CE

For: SMOOTH TRANSITION

This tablet was made in Celtic England and can now be seen in the Roman Baths Museum, Bath, England.

This small stone table from Celtic England represents the three ages of woman, from maiden to crone. It may speak to you if you are going through a transitional period in your life or are trying to adjust to a major change. You may, perhaps, be experiencing a troubled relationship with your mother, daughter or grandmother. Or, you may be a first-time mother or grandmother and feeling the effect that an extra generation in your family has on you.

Celtic Symbolism of Three

Women in groups of three have been significant throughout the ages in the art of female spirituality. For the ancient Greeks, all life was like a thread spun by a sacred female trio. One goddess spun the thread, one measured it out and one chose when to break it off.

When the sacred female trio was first depicted by the ancient Celts under Roman rule, it appealed to women as well as soldiers, merchants and officials when they were far from home. It symbolized the pleasures of family life, the power of women and the thought that divine hands which rocked the cradle might also rule the world.

The number three also had a powerful symbolism for the Celts. Their art is characterized by 'triplism'. The three mothers were known as the 'Matronae' and were often the mother goddesses of specific territories.

Sacred female trios – as the tablet opposite shows – sit or stand side by side and are fully clothed. They often have children on their laps or baskets of fruit, loaves or fishes. In some instances a breast is bared and an infant is being suckled. In others, swaddling bands and baby-washing equipment are shown. In one example, they spin thread like the goddesses of fate in ancient Greece.

Three Stages of Life

The transition from the maiden phase to the mother phase is triggered by the start of menstruation. The transition from the mother phase to the crone phase is triggered by the stopping of menstruation. The female life is three-in-one, a trinity, a sacred trio.

In some sacred female trios, the figures are identical. In others, the figures differ from each other. The three phases of female life are shown to illustrate the progression from maiden to mother to crone. These phases correspond to the phases of the moon. The new moon is the crescent moon of the maiden. It waxes to the full moon of the mother, then wanes to the crescent moon of the crone.

In the maiden phase the woman is single, strong, growing. She is full of hope, enthusiasm, potential. Her whole future lies ahead of her. She is ripe for passion and ecstasy. She is ready to open herself to the possibilities of her life. She

is admired. Her strength has yet to be tested and she looks forward to the challenges ahead.

Her youthful beauty and unself-conscious flirting may get her into trouble. The world is full of sexual predators and potential fathers for her children. She is surrounded by choices. She is wonderful. She is powerful. But she is also vulnerable. So much of what she does is life-shaping, forms her fate.

In the mother phase the woman conceives and gives birth to children, to accomplishments great and small, to creative projects seen and unseen. She nests, nurtures, plans, protects, manages, takes responsibility. She gives away much of herself to others.

To successfully conceive, carry and give birth to a baby makes a woman a mother and is a cause for celebration. But the glory of motherhood is haunted by the spectres of pain, injury and death in childbirth, of still-born babies, infant mortality, miscarriages, unwanted pregnancies, abortions, infertility and the mundane hurt and messiness of menstruation. All women have to face and cope with these spectres in their heroic mother phase. Biological mothers often have to sacrifice their own potential to fulfil their mothering role. They will be loved but they have to be energetic, patient and endlessly creative to function as a mother. They have to be particularly brave and wise as their children grow up and leave them. Much mothering is also undertaken by foster and adoptive mothers, godmothers, aunts, teachers, nurses and carers. The mother phase of female life is about fullness of life and fruition.

In the crone phase the woman enjoys a release from the sexual imperatives which have gripped her since she was a maiden. She enjoys a new-found freedom. She can appreciate masculine charms with little risk of being ensnared by them. She acquires a new clarity of vision. She can harvest the fruits of her labours. She has seen life in its stark simplicity. This gives her a distinctive sparkiness.

She knows sorrow and contentment. She is feared. Her knowledge is often denied and her wisdom derided. But she has energy now for herself now. Her life is her own and she knows the secret of peace. She begins to disappear, to be less needed by others, more self-sufficient. She bears the burden of memory but also has the gift of time, for a while.

MAKE YOUR ✳ ✳ ✳ Easy

Sacred Trio

Carve your trio as a relief to resemble the original as much as possible. When making this relief, bear in mind the differing ages and states of the three figures. The female on the left is the youngest, the most vibrant of the three. The mother figure in the middle should appear boldest and strongest and at the height of her powers. The crone on the right is almost fading away and looks smaller than the mother figure. Although the original has been damaged and the figures no longer have all their original facial features, you may like to add your own personal touch to your relief and give them your personality. As with all the goddesses, each one will be individual to you and reflect your personality.

YOU WILL NEED

- *Chopping board to work on*
- *Rolling pin*
- *Pencil*
- *Modelling tool*
- *Kitchen knife*
- *Water*

1 Using a rolling pin, roll the whole piece of clay until it is about 1 cm (½in) thick. If your clay is very wet leave to dry out for half an hour or so, until it is easier to mould.

2 Use the sharp end of the modelling tool or a pencil and begin to carve the left-hand figure (see page 68), the maiden. Notice that she has one foot showing beneath a pleated skirt.

3 Do exactly the same for the central mother figure. Note that her hands and arms seem to clasped and folded across her breasts and she has two feet clearly visible.

Step 4

4 Lastly, draw out the shape of the wise older woman on your right. This figure is fading away and is slightly smaller than the maiden. This part of the relief has been damaged. You may restore her if you wish.

5 Wait until the clay is fairly hard in texture, then begin to carve out the three figures. Take your modelling tool, or use the flat blade of a knife, to gouge or carve the clay from the drawn outline of each figure. Carefully scrape the clay away from the neck, head, foot and skirt area of each figure. Do not scrape away too much, however, or the tablet itself will become too thin.

The result should be three figures standing proud from the clay as

Step 5

if they have been carved out of stone. If the clay is tearing or your tools skidding across the clay then it is too wet to work with and must be left to dry for half an hour or so.

6 To complete your Sacred Trio, add the details of the pleats in their skirts and their eyes and noses. The mother's features should stand out the most strongly and proudly, whilst the maiden looks to be growing in strength, and the crone fading away.

Step 6

7 Smooth down with water or, if you prefer, leave a rougher surface to mimic the surface of the original stone.

8 As this is a flat model, you may like to make a round hole at the top before the clay is dry, so that the finished tablet can be hung on a wall.

73

Reflect on Your Sacred Trio

Lie down or sit in a relaxed position, close your eyes and focus in your imagination on yourself in the virgin phase of your life. Honour the maiden that you are or once were.

Imagine yourself travelling back in time to the early history of the British Isles when the land was covered in unexplored forest. You arrive in the virgin forest. This is a fertile, fruitful place. The forest has grown, the trees have multiplied because it has taken life into itself and been transformed, giving birth and taking dead things back to be recycled.

Feel the moss under your fingertips, breathe deeply the scent of damp grass, herbs and lush vegetation. With your mind's eye, scan the forest. There are no paths here, no trace of other humans. You are the first. Great peace surrounds you. All you can hear is the buzzing of bees and a powerful, yet gentle, chorus of bird-song. Small shafts of light cut through the dense foliage to the earth. The light plays on your face and warms your body.

Breathe in the tranquillity, peace, warmth, light and pristine scent of this place. Take it all inside you and hold it there. On the out breath, exhale all the polluting noise and fumes of city life. Breathe in again the growth all around you. Remember the strength and freshness of your own lush and juicy energy, poised, waiting, preparing to open up to new experiences.

You may rest in between phases of the meditation if you need to. When you are ready, move on to the mother and fighter phase. The female must fight throughout her life to protect her freedom and dignity, to protect herself. But the mother phase makes the greatest demands on her heroic resources. In this phase the woman stands up fiercely for what she sees as right. She battles to give birth to creative projects or children.

Look at the mother figure you have carved. Think back over your most difficult moments when you have fought for what you knew to be right. Acknowledge how you felt afterwards, perhaps a little shaky, but liberated because you did not back down.

Remember the joys of mother-hood. If you are in the mother phase at the moment, dwell on the joy which beams through the trials and tribulations. If you are in the maiden phase, think of the challenges and rewards which await you.

Breathe deeply and let yourself fill with confidence and strength. Breathe out negative self doubt and in to celebrate the fullness you have from the mother figure.

Now move on to the crone phase. She has independence and is freed from menstrual pain and bleeding. In your crone phase – actual or imagined – notice the changes in your energy. Remember the crone you have carved. Concentrate your energy and use your wisdom to realize what you really want to do and be.

The crone's gifts are spinning, weaving and divination. Knowing the past and sensing the future. Imagine looking up into the dark summer night. The infinite colour of the sky is yours, the darkness which extends is full of millions of bright stars and planets. Breathe in all this space. See the shooting stars which show your bursts of energy. Nearby a bonfire burns. The sparks fly high into the night air. These sparks are your ideas and wishes, your talents, your accomplishments, your moments of bliss, your perspective on life. You travel out into infinity.

75

Xochiquetzal

CENTRAL AMERICA, 900 CE

For: BEAUTY

This delightful figure embodying the spirit of Xochiquetzal is one of a pair of clay whistles found in Jaina Island, Mexico.

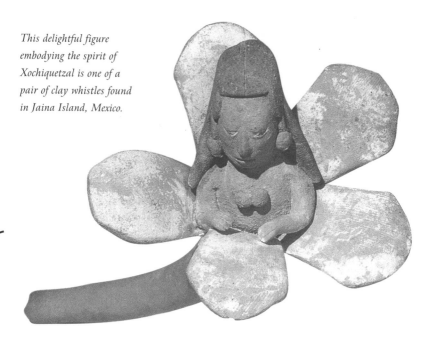

Xochiquetzal is a goddess of the Mayan civilization. Her name means 'The Precious Flower'. She is the goddess of flowers, beauty, pleasure and sexuality. With the gift of flowers she brings music and song. Her singing in springtime makes people happy. She is sometimes depicted as a butterfly sipping at the nectar of flowers.

She lives on the mountain-tops with musicians and female dancers and brings good luck to children. She is pleased whenever a woman experiences the pleasures of her body. She celebrates female sexuality as a source of erotic blossoming and spiritual transformation. Celebrate your own sexuality and beauty by making your own figurine. Feel her happiness and spirit lift you and become aware of the power of your inner beauty. Let her inspire you to bring happiness to others through your own laughter and joy.

The Laughing Maya Goddess

This figurine and the flower from which she emerges are made in the form of a clay whistle. It was found in Jaina, Mexico, and dates from the classic period of Mayan civilization, 300–900 CE. At that time there was a more or less uniform civilization throughout the Mayan lands, with great ceremonial centres such as Palenque, Tikal and Copán.

Mayan religion centred on the worship of a large number of nature gods, as we now understand from deciphering their sophisticated system of writing. The highly complex Mayan calendar was the most accurate known to humans until the introduction of the Gregorian calendar. The Mayan people domesticated the dog and the turkey, but had no draught animals or wheeled vehicles.

They produced fine pottery and their techniques of spinning, dyeing and weaving cotton were highly perfected. Cacoa beans and copper bells served as currency. Copper was also used for personal ornamentation. So too were gold, silver, jade, shells and colourful plumage.

The facial expression of the goddess depicted in this clay whistle may be somewhat solemn but figures have been found in the Veracruz area which have wide grins and ecstatic faces. They are known as 'The Laughing Goddesses' and were probably modelled on priestesses dedicated to 'The Precious Flower', the goddess Xochiquetzal.

Rituals of the Goddess

In ancient rituals to honour Xochiquetzal, young people dressed as butterflies and humming-birds. They built a bower of roses and danced around her image as the goddess of love and delight. They let loose their youthful high spirits for her.

A delightful story about the humming-bird dates from Mayan times. One day the goddesses set a challenge to a human woman. Who has the most beautiful pubic hair? The woman conjured up a humming-bird on the advice of her animal guardian. The humming-bird plucked the feathery down from her brightly coloured breast and carefully wove it into the woman's pubic hair. With this help from the humming-bird the woman outshone even the goddesses for her pubic hair was gloriously the most beautiful.

Flower Goddesses around the World

The spirit of Xochiquetzal is evident far beyond Mayan civilization – beauty is celebrated the world over and all through history. In ancient Sumer girls sang 'Our breasts stand up! Our pubic hair is grown!' when they acted as a chorus of bridesmaids accompanying the goddess Inana to her wedding bed and bridegroom. In mid-twentieth century London, skipping schoolgirls chanted together:

On the mountain stands a lady
Who she is I do not know,
All she wants is gold and silver,
All she wants is a nice young man!

In Welsh mythology the flower maiden is the archetype of the adolescent girl. Like a blossom in springtime, she is intense and vibrant, delicate and vulnerable. In India, too, female sexuality is associated with flowers. Celebrate this sexuality by making a figure in the spirit of the beautiful Xochiquetzal.

MAKE YOUR ✳ ✳ ✳ Challenging

Xochiquetzal

If you decide to make this figure, take special care when rolling out the long stem. It should not be too thin, as it must support the flower and the goddess at the end. You could also alter the facial expression of the figure to give her a more mischievous look, as this is commonly seen in goddesses of this kind.

YOU WILL NEED

- *Chopping board to work on*
- *Kitchen knife*
- *Modelling tool*
- *Water*

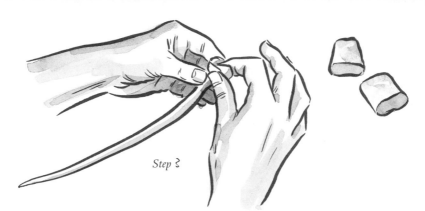

Step 3

1 Using the knife, cut the clay into three pieces of equal size.

2 Roll out a long sausage of clay for the stem. As you roll, press more heavily on one end of the sausage, so that it is tapered slightly.

Step 4

79

3 At the other end of the sausage, pinch out the clay and open up to allow for the addition of petals.

4 Using the knife, cut the second piece of clay into five even petal shapes. Press them flat on to the table to form the basic petals.

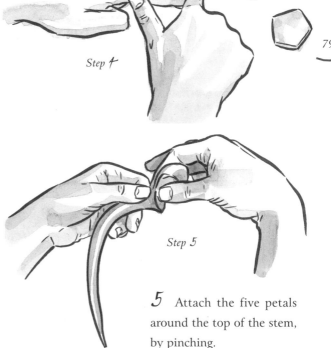

Step 5

5 Attach the five petals around the top of the stem, by pinching.

6 Mould the petals together to look like a blooming flower, then smooth them down with your fingertips dipped into water. When the flower is complete, set it aside while you make the figurine to sit inside it.

8 Chop three small strips from the second piece of clay for the arms, breasts and hair. Leave one larger piece, which will later be used for the head.

9 Take the first strip and divide it into two equal parts. Roll each into a ball and join to the torso as Xochiquetzal's breasts. Use your modelling tool to mould the final breast shape and to smooth down a join between the breasts and the body.

Step 6

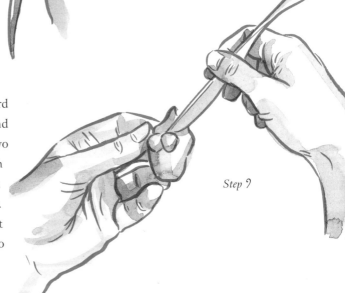

7 Take the third piece of clay and break it into two equal pieces. With one piece, fashion a short rounded torso. Pinch the clay at one end of the torso to form a neck.

Step 9

10 Roll the other two strips into slim sausages to use as arms. Attach them at the back of the torso, and then curve them round to the front of the body. Mould the ends of the arms into hand shapes and bring them into a prayer-like pose.

Step 10

11 Roll the larger piece of the remaining clay into an oval head shape. Attach to the pointed neck shape on the body using your modelling tool to smooth down the join and create a neck.

12 As you work on Xochiquetzal, check that she will fit into the flower head you have created. Make adjustments as you go along to ensure she is the right size.

13 Break of a small piece from the last strip of clay and set aside. Flatten the last strip of clay and smooth into an oval shape, which can be draped over the head to form the hair (see page 22). Smooth down at the back and use the modelling tool to create the right shape.

14 Use the last of the clay to add final details, moulding a nose on the face and drawing on the eyes and mouth with your tool or a pencil. You may also like to add earrings and more detail to her hair.

81

Step 14

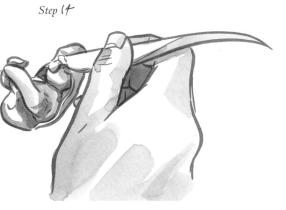

15 Finally, place Xochiquetzal into her flower. Wet the inside of the flower and the base of her torso before placing her so that she remains in position. Use your modelling tool to smooth the join between the base of the flower and the figurine. so that she will be secure once dry.

Step 15

Reflect on Your Xochiquetzal

This is an extract from Romeo and Juliet *by William Shakespeare, taken from a scene in which Juliet's parents have proposed that she be married, aged fourteen. Her nurse remembers her as a toddler and realizes how quickly she has become a maiden, ripe for sexual fulfilment.*

For she could stand high lone;
    nay, by the rood,
She could have run and waddled
    all about;
For even the day before, she broke
    her brow;
And then my husband – God be
    with his soul!
A' was a merry man – took up the
    child:
'Yea,' quoth he, 'dost though fall
    upon thy face?
Thou wilt fall backward when
    thou hast more wit;

Wilt thou not, Jule?' and by my
    halidom,
The pretty wretch left crying, and
    said 'Ay'.
To see how a jest shall come
about!
I warrant, an I should live a
    thousand years,
I should never forget it: 'Wilt thou
    not, Jule?'
And, pretty fool, it stinted and
said
'Ay'.

Romeo and Juliet, *William Shakespeare, Act I, Scene III*

Prajnaparamita

CAMBODIA, 1200 CE

For: WISDOM

This strong and peaceful image is a representation of Prajnaparamita or 'Perfect Wisdom'. The Buddha in her headdress indicates higher consciousness. She is inward looking, with a pious and meditative expression. The gently spreading smile on her smooth, passion-free face reveals the distinctive quality of Buddhist spirituality. Her long ears are signs of her wisdom. Her posture demonstrates persistent patience.

Prajnaparamita may be relevant to you if you seek peace and inner wisdom in your life. Meditating upon this figurine will induce a feeling of calm and lasting joy in a world too often filled with noise and meaningless action.

Prajnaparamita was first mentioned in Buddhist literature two thousand years ago in *The Perfection of Wisdom in 8,000 Lines*. She is not a saviour to whom one can appeal, but a vision of that which is sought and an image to focus on during meditation.

This statue is now in the Museum of Asiatic Arts in Paris, France. She originally came from Angkor in Cambodia.

The sacred texts of ancient India were written in Sanskrit and their word for 'wisdom' is feminine. Prajnaparamita is a feminine personification of wisdom. However, she is not worshipped and is rarely represented as an icon. Her major qualifications are lightness, emptiness, space and an expression both clinical and compassionate. She is elusive. She is not possessed by anyone, but she absorbs all. It is this feeling that you may experience when you place her on your altar and meditate.

Femininity and Wisdom

The pursuit of wisdom personified as feminine is a major metaphor and spiritual discipline in Buddhism. Prajnaparamita is the mother of the Buddhas and also the desired lover. The male Buddhist student is often compared to a man in love. In his constant contemplation of wisdom he is like someone always thinking of his beloved, especially when separated from her. In his readiness to experience enlightenment he is like a pregnant woman about to give birth. In his practice of compassion for all beings he is like the mother of an only child in his attentive care.

Buddhism holds that salvation from suffering lies only in our own efforts. The Buddha himself taught that in understanding how we create suffering for ourselves we can become free. The way of the Buddha spread from his native India throughout the Far East to become the dominant religion in many Eastern countries. The Buddha now has many followers in the West.

Rise of the Buddha

Legend tells us that the young Buddha, being brought up as a prince, became increasingly dissatisfied with the futility of sensual delights. At the age of twenty-nine he renounced his wealth, shaved his head and donned the coarse robe of a wandering ascetic. One night as he sat in deep meditation beneath a sacred fig tree at Gaya, he experienced Supreme Enlightenment. For the next forty-five years he travelled around northern India teaching his religion of wisdom, enlightenment and compassion.

Six centuries after his death, a pantheon of celestial Buddhas was developed, two of which acknowledged the feminine principle. Kuan-Yin, personification of compassion, was one and the other was Prajnaparamita.

85

MAKE YOUR ✳ ✳ ✳ Challenging

Prajnaparamita

Although this ancient sculpture is broken, antique and incomplete examples of faith are still used today to focus meditation. The instructions do not attempt to mend the sculpture, although you could build up the arms if you wanted a complete figure. Features to particularly focus on include the calm, serene expression on her face. Notice the curved shape of the torso. Her eyes are closed. The headdress, although quite small, is decorated with a Buddha effigy.

YOU WILL NEED

- *Chopping board to work on*
- *Modelling tool*
- *Water*
- *Kitchen knife*
- *Pencil*
- *Thread or textured fabric (optional)*

1 Cut a 2-cm (¾-in) slice from your lump of clay. This should be enough to add details including the ears, headdress, nose and shoulders of the figurine. Wrap this piece in plastic to keep it malleable and set to one side to work on later.

2 Roll the rest of the clay into a thick sausage shape, standing roughly 12 cm (5 in) tall. This one piece will be moulded to form the whole figure.

3 At the top of your figure start to shape the head by squeezing the neck and building the shoulders.

Step 3

Step 4

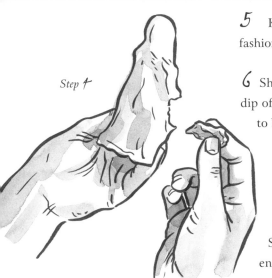

5 Keep on working the shape to fashion a neat waist and small breasts.

6 Shape the knees and emphasize the dip of the lap by adding slithers of clay to build up the skirt and legs.

7 At the back of the figure use your modelling tool or knife to draw on the shape of the legs of the figure folded under. Smooth the base of the model to ensure that she sits comfortably on a flat surface.

4 Break small pieces from the top of the cylinder and add them to the bottom to build the area which will become hips, bottom, thighs, knees and legs tucked under.

Step 7

Step 6

8 Using some of the clay set aside in step 1, roll a small sausage and mould it into a cone of clay for the headdress.

9 Next, add small raisins to the side of the head, wetting them, if necessary, to make them stick. Shape into the elongated ears.

Step 13

10 Add a small piece of clay for the nose. Use the modelling tool to smooth and mould it into the desired shape.

Step 9

11 When you are happy with the shape of the nose, shape the face and draw in the serene smiling mouth and the closed eyes of the figure with a pencil or the sharp end of the modelling tool.

12 Complete the other details by drawing in the necklace, cleavage and the waistband of the skirt. If you want the details to be more subtle, smooth them over slightly using water.

13 The remaining details are optional. You may use the rest of your clay to build up the layers of Prajnaparamita's hairstyle if you wish, drawing on the details of the hair with a pencil. You may also add on a small piece of clay for the Buddha figure on her headdress (see outline above, left). If this proves too fiddly, however, draw the shape on.

14 Finally, use your modelling tool to score the zig-zag pattern into the lap of the skirt. Then, if you wish to make a more intricate design, take the piece of thread or fabric and press it into the clay of the central panel of the skirt area. You can choose a pattern of your own for this, or try to recreate a plain woven cotton texture.

Step 14

89

Reflect on Your Prajnaparamita

There is something beyond our mind,
which abides in silence within our mind.
It is the supreme mystery beyond thought.
Let one's mind and one's subtle body rest upon that
and not rest on anything else.

Sacred text from ancient India

Sheelagh-na-gig

IRELAND, 1200 CE

For: FEMALE SPIRIT

A sheelagh-na-gig is a carving of a crone displaying her genitalia and holding open her vagina. Sheelagh-na-gigs were made as lasting reminders in stone of female sexuality and the facts of human reproduction. Often placed over the entrance to churches built between 1100 and 1400 CE France, England and

Ireland, this display of female genitalia was believed to ward off the devil. In those days it was said a woman could stop a mad bull in its tracks by baring her bottom! Some sheelagh-na-gigs were placed over church entrances where weddings took place. The bride and groom could touch the sheelagh-na-gig, scrape dust from it and take away the dust to bring them fertility.

A Celebration of Sexuality

You may like to make your own sheelagh-na-gig and use her ancient strength to cast a web of protection around yourself and your home. She may also be made as a celebration of your own sexuality and to aid fertility. She shows that you are proud of your femaleness and the power it can convey.

Sheelagh-na-gigs can be shocking even today. One of the funniest and most famous is to be found in Kilpeck church in Herefordshire, England. Other examples have their ribs exposed and tattoos on their faces and upper bodies. Some are smiling. Others brandish discs, sticks or horns and look aggressive or hostile.

Symbols of Fertility

Sheelagh-na-gigs first appeared at a time when vast areas of forest were being cleared in Europe for agriculture. The discovery at this time of ancient 'Venus' figurines made by stone-age farmers may have inspired them. Like the older carvings, the sheelagh-na-gigs illustrate the mysteries of female anatomy. They also symbolized the earth's fertility and the need to take care of it.

They were first carved in France in the twelfth century CE and brought to England and Ireland by Christian pilgrims. Sheelagh-na-gigs were carved for nearly three hundred years, particularly in Ireland, where most surviving examples are to be found. They followed the folk tradition of warrior goddesses and the Celtic hag, Morrigan, who becomes a beautiful young woman when kings and heroes reluctantly make love to her.

Not only churches, but other important buildings, such as mills, had

This Sheelagh-na-gig was found in Ballylarkin, in County Kilkenny, Ireland. She was carved in about 1200 CE and is now in the National Museum in Dublin, Ireland.

91

sheelagh-na-gigs installed to protect them. The main purpose of the sheelagh-na-gigs may have been to suppress the sexual desires of the clergy.

In the twelfth century the cult of celibacy became increasingly important within the Christian church. Monks and priests were very strictly bound by their vows to avoid sex. The hag-like, hostile sheelagh-na-gig may well have been intended by the church authorities as a repulsive warning to assist with the keeping of those vows!

In the nineteenth century the term sheelagh-na-gig was applied to any woman whom a man could pay for a display of female genitalia to avert his ill-luck. At this time, the medieval carvings in churches became a source of

embarrassment for the clergy. Some were removed and those which were left in place were rarely mentioned in church guide-books.

In the twenty-first century the role of the sheelagh-na-gigs in the art of female spirituality can be better appreciated. Their power sings across the centuries. In the church of Ballyvourney near Killarney in Ireland, Christian pilgrims recently performed a ritual of devotion to the female saint Gobnat. It included touching the sheelagh-na-gig installed on a lintel above the church's medieval window.

Create your own sheelagh-na-gig as a counterblast to medieval Christian condemnation of women and their sexuality. Celebrate your female spirit.

MAKE YOUR　　　　✳ ✳ ✳ Easy
Sheelagh-na-gig

By following the step-by-step instructions you will achieve something which looks as close to the original as possible. If, however, you prefer to experiment, you could make the figure three dimensional and stand up on her own. Whichever way you choose, notice particularly the thickness of her neck and her facial features and her thin body, showing ribs on either side.

YOU WILL NEED

- *Chopping board to work on*
- *Rolling pin*
- *Pencil*
- *Modelling tool*
- *Water*

Step 4

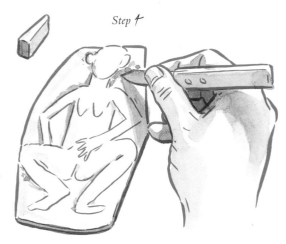

1 Break off a grape-sized piece of clay and set aside for the head, as it is raised higher than the rest of the carving.

2 Using the rolling pin, roll the remaining piece of clay into a rectangular block roughly 1 cm (½ in) thick. It should measure about 10 cm by 15 cm (4 in by 6 in).

working on the outline until the figure is raised from the background, forming a relief.

93

3 Draw with a pencil or the modelling tool the outline of the sheelagh, using the original on page 90 or the completed models on page 95 as your guide.

4 Gouge out the clay around the figure, saving the pieces you've chiselled off to build up the body and neck of the sheelagh. Keep

Step 5

5 Mould the pieces you have set aside into small raisin shapes, and use them to build up the body, arms and legs of the sheelagh. Smooth the figure down with a little water as you go along.

6 Take the clay set aside earlier for the head. Build up the head and chin to make it slightly more prominent than the body.

7 Use two small clay raisins for the ears and two tiny oval shapes for eyes. Once applied to the figure, use the modelling tool to create the strong features of the sheelagh-na-gig's face.

8 To complete the face, add a small strip of clay for the nose, then draw in the brows and mouth with a pencil or the modelling tool.

9 Finally, using your pencil or modelling tool, complete the sheelagh-na-gig by carving small pendulous breasts, the fingers of both hands and the vulva and clitoris. If you have any clay left over, build up these features so they stand proud from the relief.

10 The whole model can then be smoothed over with some water on your fingertips. If you wish it to be more like the original, you could make rough markings with the tool or press something with a rough texture into the clay (see page 125).

Step 8

11 Once your relief is completed and before it has dried, you may like to cut out a small hole some-where near the top of the piece. When she is dry you could then hang her over a doorway, as was the tradition with sheelagh-na-gigs. Alternatively, fix her to a wall around which you can build your altar, to meditate on her and the powers she imbues and brings forth in you.

Reflect on Your Sheelagh-na-gig

95

This piece of ancient Celtic prose tells of a woman choosing her husband and celebrating the physical aspect of love. Here she summons the knight, Elil:

'Rise, wonderful Elil. Thou shalt have rest, bravest of the brave. Put your hand around my neck to begin the joy of love. Blessed is the gift of love when men and women kiss. If that should not suffice for thee, excellent knight, I'll give of myself from knee to navel to heal the pangs of love.'

Fertility and Good Luck
This is what to say when you touch a sheelagh-na-gig and scrape dust from her to bring you fertility and good luck:

I call upon the shape of all,
Touchstone of truthful witness,
This is where I am coming from,
This is where I am going.

Pathway Icon

INDIA, MODERN

For: FERTILITY

The ancient tradition of Goddess worship in India flourishes today in temples, and in the art of the Hindu pathway icons. These icons are set by the roadside to denote a sacred space and to be a focus of religion, cult and local mythology. Traditionally, the important events of life such as birth, marriage and death are occasions for the making and worship of pathway icons. In India, it is normal and commonplace to create your own goddess as a pathway

This modern-day wayside shrine in Rajasthan, India, shows a god, Bhaivara, and a Mother Goddess. The simple altar on which they are set up includes a bell, a conch-shell, incense and holy water.

icon like the one shown opposite. These can take many different forms, and this is but one example. You may choose to make your own Mother Goddess Pathway Icon for such a reason. Perhaps you have recently celebrated a marriage or a birth in the family, or you would like to mark a day which is important to you in a spiritual way.

In India, home-made icons are placed beside a path, beneath a tree, at a crossroads, on the bank of a river or in the corner of a house. They embody the fears, hopes, needs and beliefs of millions of people. Their basic shapes are often abstract and can seem very modern, but they are made in a tradition stretching back to antiquity.

They are anointed, clothed and decorated like temple deities. Flowers and incense are offered to them. They are archetypes which emerge from individual consciousness and re-enter the collective subconscious.

Creation as Worship

Pathway icons are deeply rooted in local tradition and play an important role in the daily life of village communities. In this culture, life, art and religion are not compartmentalized. Creating a work of art is an act of worship. The act of creation is a process inspired by a desire to discover the divine, to make visible the invisible, to make known the unknown, to give form to the formless.

Creating a work of art as an act of worship is a way of knowing the workings of the inner self and reaching the point where artist and mystic become one. Indian mythology, metaphysics and mysticism cannot be separated. There is an underlying connection between the highest philosophical knowledge in religious texts and the simple spiritual life of a village community.

Traditionally, the decorated figures recognizable as deities with heads, arms, legs, ears, eyes and tongues have beside them a cryptic symbol or abstract form. There can come a point during the worship of the figurative deities when devotion switches to the abstract symbol to convey a state of feeling. Squares, circles, triangles, spirals and ovals can all represent the divine.

Some pathway icons consist of geometric shapes cut from silver, gold, green or red tin foil and pasted on to rocks, trees or walls. Each geometric shape may be an individual offering by

97

a newly-wed or childless couple. Often an abstract icon has a pair of eyes. Eyes bring about mystical union between the passive icon and the active worshipper.

These icons are often made from local materials such as clay, straw, stone, bamboo or fabric and set on a lime-washed platform. Both the icon and the place where it is set are sanctified by rituals and the chanting of mantras. From this moment of sanctification the icon ceases to be a piece of clay, straw, stone, bamboo or fabric and becomes a manifestation of the divine principle.

It is believed that the goddess brings forth life and all that exists. At the end of the cosmic cycle she destroys all creation. She absorbs the negative aspects of life and thereby makes way for new life. The cycle of creation and destruction that the goddess represents is fundamental to nature.

MAKE YOUR ✳ ✳ ✳ Easy

Pathway Icon

The body shape of the Pathway Icon is the easiest to make of all the goddess-figures, as it is made from one simple form. This model differs from the others in that its decoration is needed to complete the model. She is painted an earthy shade of red to make it like the icons seen in India. Red is the colour representing Shakti (see page 62). The foil to make the veil and the paint are applied once the model is dry.

YOU WILL NEED

- Chopping board to work on
- Modelling tool
- Pencil
- Water
- Red, black and white poster or powder paint
- Water-based glue
- Paintbrush
- Aluminium baking foil
- Gold foil (candy or chocolate wrappers can be used)

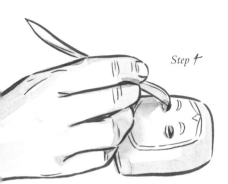

Step 4

1 Take up your clay and break off two small pieces the size of your thumbnail. Roll these into ovals to create the eyes. Set these aside wrapped in plastic, to be applied to the body later.

2 Press or roll the clay into an ovoid shape and flatten it at one end by standing it on the table. You can make the back of this figurine flat so that it can lean against a wall when finished.

3 With your modelling tool or pencil, draw on the clay the positions of the veil, eyes and eyebrows of your goddess.

4 Dig out two small oval shapes in the clay where the eyes are to go using your modelling tool.

5 Wet the clay slightly and press in the two eye shapes. Then, draw the pupils and eyebrow shapes on to the clay. Before decorating your icon, leave to dry – this may take a few days.

Step 5

6 Paint the whole face, apart from the eyes, red. To get a durable and authentic red you can add some glue to red powder paint, mix together and apply (see pages 122–125).

99

7 To complete the painting, add in the whites of the eyes and the pupils.

Step 7

Step 9

8 Cut two small half-moon shapes from the aluminium foil for the eyebrows. Stick them in position using the glue.

Step 11

9 Next, create the headdress. To do this cut tiny triangles from one side of a long strip of the aluminium baking foil. Stick in position around the face with glue.

10 Cut a small diamond shape from the gold foil for a bindi and stick in position in the centre of her forehead.

11 To make the veil, cut strips of gold foil to fit around the sides and top of the goddess, and across the bottom of her face. Use the photograph on page 96 as your reference for how she should look.

12 When you are happy with the positioning of the gold foil, stick it in position with some glue.

13 When your icon is finished and you want to display her or place her on your altar, put a garland of flowers of the season, held together like a daisy chain, around her neck.

Step 12

14 As the pathway goddesses in India come in many shapes and sizes, you could experiment with variations on this basic model. Options include changing her shape and facial features and painting her different colours.

Reflect on Your Pathway Icon

That power who exists in all
   beings as consciousness,
Reverence to her, reverence to her.
That power who exists in all beings
   as reason,
Reverence to her, reverence to her.
That power who exists in all beings
   as energy,
Reverence to her, reverence to her.
That power who exists in all beings
   as peace,
Reverence to her, reverence to her.

That power who exists in all beings
   as memory,
Reverence to her, reverence to her.
That power who exists in all beings
   as fulfilment,
Reverence to her, reverence to her.
That power who exists in all beings
   as mother
Reverence to her, reverence to her.
That power who exists in all beings
   as illusion
Reverence to her, reverence to her.
Reverence to her, reverence to her.

Hymn to the Great Mother Goddess recited during her festival

Akua'ba

For: **A HEALTHY, BEAUTIFUL BABY**

Akua'ba dolls are made by the Ashanti people of Ghana, Africa. These examples are now in a private collection in New York.

An Akua'ba is a beautiful moon-faced female figure, which the Ashanti women of west Africa traditionally carry around with them or wear in jewellery form.

The name Akua'ba means 'child of Akua'. According to legend, Akua was a woman who carried one of these figures. She became pregnant and gave birth to a beautiful baby. From that time onwards, women from that part of the world have carried these figurines – usually carved from wood – in the hopes of conceiving and bearing a beautiful and healthy child like that of Akua.

The hopes of women have ever been the same the world over, whatever their cultural differences. Women everywhere hope that their children will be born healthy and beautiful.

If the sentiment behind Akua'ba is relevant to you and your time of life right now, make your own version and use her power to your advantage. You may choose her if you, or someone you know, is expecting a baby, or if you are hoping to conceive and want to wish for a healthy, beautiful child.

An Act of Magic

Traditionally an Akua'ba is carried as an act of magic, to make things happen by means of the carrier's thoughts and symbolic actions. For these reasons, you may dress your Akua'ba in scraps of material or adorn her with jewellery to reflect your feelings and hopes for your unborn child.

The fact that all life depends on the female and her moon cycle is reflected in the serene face of the Akua'ba. The flat round face, high forehead, small mouth and long neck form an ideal of female beauty. Gaze upon the face of your Akua'ba to transmit its perfect beauty to the baby inside your womb.

Osun the Female God

The importance of the female is told in a story of the Yoruba people of west Africa. In this culture the supreme creator, Olodumare, is both female and male. Olodumare wanted to prepare the earth for human habitation and sent the seventeen major deities to organize things. Only one of them, Osun, was female. Each of the deities was given special powers and functions. The male deities held meetings and made important decisions, but they excluded Osun because she was female.

However, Osun's powers and functions were too important to be ignored. Like all women, her womb is the matrix of all life in the universe. In her lies unlimited potential and the infinities of existence. With her beaded comb she parts the pathway of both human and divine life. She leads all the powerful beings and forces in the world. Therefore, when she was ignored by the male deities, their plans failed. They had to turn to Olodumare for help.

Olodumare told the gods to go back to Osun, make a sacrifice to her, beg her forgiveness and to give her whatever she wanted.

The male deities did as they were told and Osun forgave them. She asked for, and received, the secret knowledge they had used to exclude her. From then on their plans were successful.

103

MAKE YOUR   ✴ ✴ ✴ Moderate

Akua'ba

When you are modelling your Akua'ba, take particular care with the head. It is very large in proportion with the body and may need extra support at the back. Do not worry if she does not stand up alone. This figure is a comfortable shape to hold in your hand as you meditate. Bring your own personality to your Akua'ba. Do not feel you have to copy the facial features or neck decoration of the original slavishly. This is your own personal goddess. Make her unique.

YOU WILL NEED

- *Chopping board to work on*
- *Ruler*
- *Modelling tool*
- *Pencil*

1 Cut the clay in half and set one piece aside, wrapped in plastic.

2 Break the other piece in half again and roll one of the pieces into a ball for the face of your Akua'ba. The rest will be used for adding detail.

3 Squash the ball flat with your hands until it is about 10 cm (4 in) in diameter. Set the head aside wrapped in plastic to keep it workable.

4 Take up the larger piece set aside in step 1 and roll it into a cylinder shape to form the torso of Akua'ba. Taper the sausage slightly at one end by applying more pressure there, to make the neck.

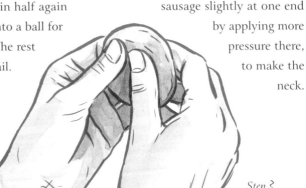

Step 3

5 To make the arms, take up three quarters of the piece of clay left from step 2. Roll into a sausage about 10 cm (4 in) in length. Cut in two and attach an arm to either side of the body.

6 Once in position, squeeze the end of each arm to bring it to a point.

Step 5

7 Use the leftover clay from step 5 to roll small balls of clay to form the breasts and belly button. Apply and smooth the join.

9 When you have completed the neck make a point at the top.

8 Form the neck rings by scoring into the clay all round the neck then building it up between each score or ring. If you find it easier, use some extra clay to roll a sausage to wind round the neck. This can then be moulded to look like rings round the neck. Alternatively you can leave the neck bare, and when your figurine is dry, decorate her with your own beads.

Step 8

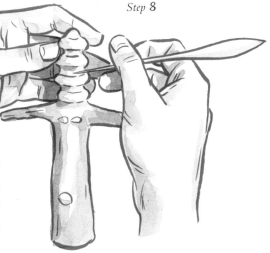

Step 10

10 Take the head and make a small hole on one side. This can then be used to attach the head to the point on the neck.

11 As the neck is long and thin, you may need to add raisins of clay at the back, to strengthen it and ensure that she can support the weight of the head. Smooth the joint with the modelling tool.

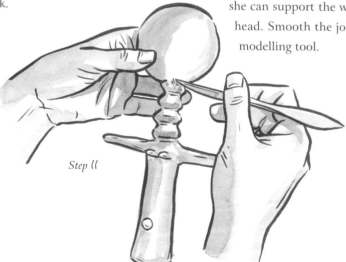

Step 11

12 To finish, draw in Akua'ba's face with a sharpened pencil. If you feel confident, build up the nose, mouth and eyebrows with small raisins of clay and mould using a small amount of water and your modelling tool.

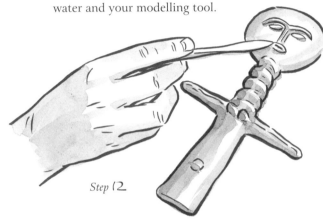

Step 12

107

Reflect on Your Akua'ba

Baby. To be or not to be?
Beautiful? Bonny?
From descendants of ancestors
You were conceived
With a cracking of twigs,
A lighting of fire.
In the void so familiar
You struggle for life.
Sleeping, kicking,

Completely unaware of what
   awaits you.
There will be smiles.
There will be an embrace
To take you through the rest,
If you can make your biggest
   journey ever.
Safely.

Fran Hazelton

Mary

BOSNIA, 1981 CE

For: A MIRACLE

Around the world Mary is recognized for her merciful, kind, soft and gentle nature. For many believers, Mary performs miracles, although she is not officially recognized as a wonder-working 'goddess'. This is particularly true for pilgrims to places famous for apparitions of Mary. One such apparition was reported on 24th June 1981 in the town of Medugorje in Bosnia, by a group of children.

They were playing near the church on a hill when the apparition made them 'nearly run out of their shoes', as one of them later recalled. They went on to have apparitions daily and subsequently on special occasions such as birthdays or at Christmas. Pilgrims now journey from many countries around the world to climb the hill of Medugorje in the hopes of seeing an apparition of Mary for themselves in this special place.

Lourdes in France is another such place. Thousands of annual pilgrimages to Mary are

This figurine is a replica of the statue of Mary which stands in a public square in the town of Medugorje in Bosnia

made there every year. In this tiny village in the Pyrenees she has been seen at least eighteen times. As her presence can be felt there, Lourdes remains one of the most popular of Christian shrines, and the most important site of miraculous healing worldwide.

Manifestation of Femininity

Mary can be seen as a manifestation of what the Chinese call 'yin'. She represents the qualities which both East and West have traditionally regarded as feminine. She is yielding, soft, gentle, receptive, merciful, humble and forgiving. Because of Mary's pivotal role in Christianity the 'feminine' has tended to be identified in Western culture solely with the female.

Mary's mythology and iconography have much in common with those of the goddesses of ancient Egypt and Mesopotamia. Images of Mary holding the baby Jesus and the crucified Christ closely resemble those of Isis holding her son Horus and mummified brother-husband, Osiris (see page 56–57). In ancient Sumer, the goddess Inana was 'Queen of Earth and Heaven'. This was echoed thousands of years later in Mary's status as 'Queen of Heaven'.

Although the conventional image of Mary is demure and sexless, throughout Europe there are ancient 'Black Virgins' which have a twinkle in the eye. Many believe they represent vestiges of the ancient reverence for female sexuality and fertility which was replaced by an ideal of virginal motherhood.

Mary and the Angel Gabriel

Pilgrimages to Mary's shrines have traditionally involved journeys which provided opportunities for women to socialize and petition the Virgin for help with problems concerning sexuality or fertility. In the gospel according to St Luke, when Mary was told by the Angel Gabriel that she was pregnant she visited her much older cousin, Elizabeth, who was also pregnant. When Elizabeth heard Mary's greeting 'the babe leapt in her womb' and she was 'filled with the Holy Spirit'.

The Four Dogmas

According to Catholic theologians, Mary should be given *hyperdulia,* or special veneration. God should be given *latria* (adoration) and saints should be given *dulia* (veneration). For believers, there are four principles about Mary

109

which must be held as articles of faith. The first two are her divine motherhood and her virginity. The third dogma, is the Immaculate Conception, which spares her all stain of original sin. The fourth dogma is her assumption, body and soul, into heaven.

Mary the God Bearer

The early church decreed that Mary was *theotokos*, or 'god bearer', and the faithful have long seen Mary as the mediator between humanity and God. Mary can fulfil this mediating role because she is a creature belonging both to heaven and to earth. She is prayed to for redress against private and public wrongs and to bestow graces of all kinds. People throughout the world still 'look into the face of Mary' for comfort in times of trouble. You may be inspired by this to make your own version of Mary to bring comfort, and perhaps a small miracle, into your life.

MAKE YOUR ✹ ✹ ✹ Moderate

Mary

When you are making Mary, take special care in the details like the folds in her veil and dress and the caring, peaceful look on her face. It is not necessary to build up the back of the figure, she can be tall and slender and not as fully rounded as many of the other figurines in this book. When moulding the figure, take care to keep her arms in proportion to her body, as they can easily appear too long.

YOU WILL NEED
- *Chopping board to work on*
- *Kitchen knife*
- *Pencil*
- *Modelling tool*
- *Rolling pin*

1 Cut one third of the clay off your main lump and set aside. Cover it with plastic to keep it workable.

2 By squeezing and pinching your main lump of clay in the palm of your

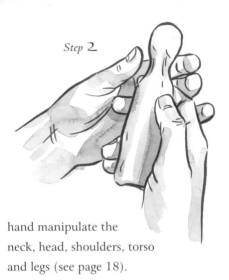

Step 2

hand manipulate the
neck, head, shoulders, torso
and legs (see page 18).

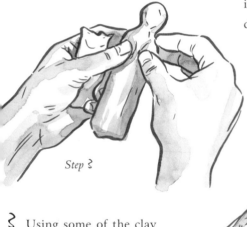

Step 3

3 Using some of the clay
set aside, gradually build
up the arms using the
squashed-raisin technique.
Keep the left arm pressed
close to the body with the
hand open. The other arm

should be bent at the elbow and pressed
against her chest. Make sure the arms
appear in proportion to her body.

4 Make a base for your figurine by
rolling a sausage from some of the
leftover clay. Wrap it round the base of
the figure to provide a support for her to
stand on.

5 Take small pieces of the clay and
stick to the base of the figure for the
rocks and flowers she is surrounded by
in the garden. If you prefer, these can be
drawn on.

111

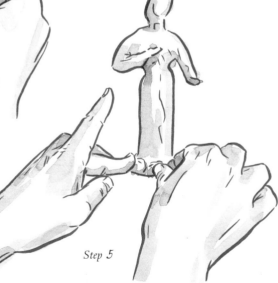

Step 5

6 Refine the shape of your Mary's face, adding a small piece of clay for the nose. Draw the eyes, brows and mouth on with a pencil (see page 21).

On the right side the veil hugs the side of the face, touches the shoulder and then fans out over the elbow.

9 Use your knife to cut the veil into shape and achieve a similar effect to the original statue.

10 Draw on details of the folds of the fabric using the modelling tool or a pencil. To finish your figurine smooth any unevenness out by applying water with your fingertips.

Step 8

7 To make Mary's veil, take a piece of clay the size of a walnut. Roll it flat with a rolling pin or press it flat with your fingers and cut into a rectangle or square. It should measure approximately 10 cm by 15 cm (4 in by 6 in).

Step 10

8 Wrap the veil over the head and smooth down, pinching at the back to create the folds. Place the veil over her left shoulder and chest so that just her hand is visible.

Reflect on Mary

Hail Mary, full of grace
Blessed art thou among women
And blessed is the fruit
Of thy womb, Jesus.
Holy Mary, Mother of God
Pray for us sinners now
And at the hour of our death.

The Hail Mary

My soul doth magnify the Lord,
And my spirit hath rejoiced in God
my Saviour.
For he hath regarded the low
estate of his handmaiden:

For, behold, from henceforth all
generations shall call me blessed.
For he who is mighty hath done to
me great things;
And holy is his name!
He hath scattered the proud in the
imagination of their hearts.
He hath put down the mighty
from their seats,
And exalted them of low degree.
He hath filled the hungry with
good things!

The Magnificat
Luke 2:46–53

Moroccan Cloth Carder

MOROCCO, MODERN

For: WORK SATISFACTION

This modern-day clay figurine originated in the mountain village of Tafza, Morocco. The woman depicted is a cloth carder who prepares fibre to be spun. She embodies a sense of accomplishment and contentment in her work. You may choose to make her if you feel that the value of your work needs to be re-affirmed by yourself and others. You may also wish to re-gain a sense of craft and skill, or a re-connection with the basic creative process.

Cloth Carding

Work such as this has been the staple work of women for centuries. Prepared fibre is spun into yarn, then woven into cloth to be dyed and sewn. It may then be embroidered with colourful silk.

This clay figurine, symbolic of women's work, was made in Morocco in modern times.

The two basic methods used to prepare fibre for spinning into thread are combing and carding. Combing is like combing tangles out of your hair. It makes the fibres lie parallel and produces strong thread. Carding is like teasing or back-combing your hair. It loosens the tangles in the fibre without combing them straight and parallel. It is done with carding paddles. The teeth of the paddles pull the fibres apart so they lie in all directions. The name comes from the Latin word for a thistle – *cardus*. In Roman times, the thorns of thistles were used for carding. These methods are still used today.

Weaving Together

Thread is spun by twisting the loosened fibres together. The thread grows out of the mass of fibres continually fed by one hand to the other. This is what the famous Venus de Milo statue was doing before she lost her arms. For millennia women have sat together spinning, weaving and sewing because these activities are compatible with childcare. They can be done at home and easily put down and resumed later. This is how communities become dependent on women for textile production.

Traditions of the Berbers

Such traditional work-patterns have remained fairly constant throughout history for the people living in the mountains of Morocco. These are the Berbers who have been in North Africa for at least 5000 years. Now a Muslim people, they mainly live in rural areas in tents or clay huts, although in the larger villages they may have stone houses. Their traditional occupations are raising sheep and cattle. They also mill flour, carve wood, and produce domestic utensils, agricultural implements, leather goods, pottery and jewellery.

The Berbers speak an ancient language called Kabyl, which is part of the Afro-Asian linguistic family. Its poetry is preserved in the voices of singing women. Each Berber village has its leading poetess, who improvises as she sings, and who is often accompanied by a drumming and singing chorus of women. One of the customary musical activities of the Berbers is that of making up a song for a new bride and performing it at the wedding feast in the village square.

Find increased work satisfaction, whatever you do, in the contentment of your own Moroccan Cloth Carder.

MAKE YOUR ✳ ✳ ✳ Challenging

Moroccan Cloth Carder

You may choose to make this figurine to give you confidence and a sense of accomplishment at work. When moulding the bottom of the figure, be sure not to press the clay too thinly, as this may cause your completed model to collapse. Note that the body can also be hollowed out to prevent it being too heavy for the bottom to support.

YOU WILL NEED

- *Chopping board to work on*
- *Kitchen knife*
- *Water*
- *Modelling tool*
- *Pencil*

1 Cut your piece of clay in half.

2 Put half back in the plastic, wrapping to keep it damp. Roll the other half into a ball.

3 To make the bottom half of your Cloth Carder, make a pinch-pot from half the clay. To do this, hold the ball of clay in one hand and, with the thumb of your other hand, push down into the middle of the ball to make a small hollow. Continue pushing down, turning the pot round as you mould it, to form the hollowed out base for your figurine.

Step 4

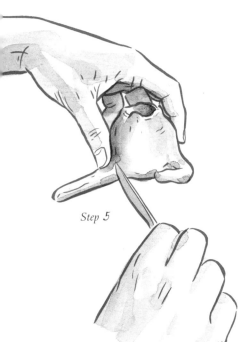

Step 5

at the front. With damp fingers smooth them into place.

6 Press the pot down to gently flatten the bottom. The base should now stand solidly supported by the crossed legs.

7 Use the rest of the clay to build the torso, head and arms of the figure. Start by cutting it in half. Roll one piece into a short squat cylinder and roughly shape the head and neck, using the pinching technique on page 18. To make it lighter, and to gain some extra clay, use your modelling tool to hollow out some of the clay from the torso.

4 Start to close in the top of the pot (which will form the waist) and pinch together as you turn until you have a small pot with a rounded bottom about 5 mm (¼ in) thick.

5 From the clay set aside in step 1, break off two pieces to make the legs. Roll into sausages and attach them at the base of the pot, sticking out at right angles, so that she looks cross-legged. Use the joining technique on page 19 to do this. Bend them back round to join

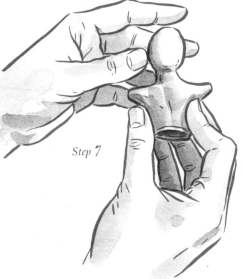

Step 7

8 Attach the body and head to the bottom of the figure. Take care to make the join between the two parts secure.

Use some wet clay smoothed down with your modelling tool to reinforce the joint if necessary.

9 Break the last piece of clay into three pieces. Divide one of these pieces into two and roll into sausages for the arms. Attach to the body in the same way as the legs.

10 Squeeze the end of the arms to create the wrists and hands, ready to hold the brushes for cloth carding.

Step 8

11 Take one of the other pieces set aside in step 9 to create the hat. The technique is the same as for the hair (see page 22). Add a small piece of clay for the top-knot.

Step 10

12 Take the remaining piece of clay and divide into three. Flatten two of the pieces into chunky squares to form the brushes.

13 Roll small sausages from the other piece of clay and add to the brushes to form the handles. Position these in the hands of

Step 13

your figurine as shown in the picture on page 114. Make sure they are firmly attached by smoothing small raisins of clay on to the join if necessary.

14 Next, add the finishing details. Use a pencil to draw in the circular breasts, the fingers, facial features (including a piece added

on for the nose), spiral dotted patterns on her body, and the bristles on the brushes. For further tips on decoration see page 124–125.

15 When you are happy with the shape of the figurine, complete her by smoothing any unevenness away with water. Leave her to dry.

119

Step 14

120

Reflect on Your Moroccan Cloth Carder

In the global economy products are manufactured and consumed by the people of the world from the raw materials of the world. Everybody is thus connected to each other, although most people living this way have no direct creative connection to the earth as their provider.

Imagine you live in a village where everything has been made by someone in your community and expresses its shared experience. Every household utensil, every item of clothing, every wall hanging, every blanket, every floor covering and perhaps even the tent you live in.

Your shoes are made from local skins. Your sweater is knitted from wool shorn from your sheep. Your evening meal is soup made from vegetables grown in nearby soil. The bowl is made from clay found in the surrounding hills. You have known the family of potters who made the bowl all your life and they have been making pottery for generations. Your mother has glazed and decorated all her pots, bowls, plates and cups using patterns and symbols which have meaning for your family, neighbours and friends. As you go to sleep at night you pull around your shoulders the blanket you wove on your loom, using the patterns learned from your mother.

Some of the patterns are like jewels and are the signs of your tribe. Some are like the houses in your village. Some are geometric shapes and look like a form of counting. Some are like crossroads. Some are like fences. Some are symbols for the trees and plants that grow all around you, for the stream running outside your home, for the hills on the far side of the valley.

All the patterns have significance and meaning for you and your people. They are your coded collective memory. They represent important events, difficult journeys, special accomplishments. They tell you who you are. They put your life in context. They connect you to your extended family in the village, to your grandparents and their grandparents. These patterns also give you roots and a sense of continuity in your life.

When you wake up in the morning you stand barefoot on the carpet which you and your sisters wove last year. It is the traditional Moroccan blue with red and black details woven through it.

Your new day begins.

Sheena Barnes

Other Media and Decoration

Although the models in this book have all been created with special non-firing modelling clay, you can experiment with many other media and ideas to make different kinds of 'goddesses' unique to you. Once you are confident working with the clay, you can experiment with your own goddess figures. Do not feel that you have to copy the instructions in this book slavishly. Neither do you have to make traditional goddesses. Seek out figures from all over the world which inspire and move you. Over the following pages are some ideas to fire your imagination.

REAL CLAY

You can use ordinary clay – terracotta is particularly attractive. As ordinary clay does not have added fibres to strengthen it, it needs to be fired in a kiln. It can then be decorated and glazed. This will provide a durable and waterproof finish.

FIMO AND SOFT MODELLING DOUGH

Fimo clays are fun to use and come in a wide range of colours, so do not need to be painted. They come in small packets so you may have to scale down the size of your figurine.

On completion the Fimo should be baked in the oven at 130°C (265°F) for twenty minutes to harden. Fimo is widely available in art and toy shops.

Soft, non-hardening children's dough is fun to work with, and can be used to practise a particularly difficult figurine. Figurines made from this material are not long-lasting, however.

CLAY FIRING

The clay included in this kit can be fired, so if you have access to a kiln this would make your figurines very strong. It can be fired at a kiln setting range of between 1000°C (1830°F) and 1250°C (2280°F). Your fired figurine can then be painted with a range of different glazes after use.

DOUGH

Dough can be used to make any of the models which do not need fine detailing, as it is quite a thick medium. The Pathway Icon or the Cycladic Grave Figure might work well. It can be made easily at home using either of the recipes below; one of which is for baked and one for uncooked dough.

Models made from dough will not be as durable and strong as those from clay, although they can be painted and varnished to strengthen them. Please remember that this dough is not edible. The cup measurement used in the recipe below can be a tea-cup or an American cup measurement; as long as you use the same cup throughout, the recipe will work. This recipe should give you enough dough to make two or three of the models in this book. If you do not use all the dough at once, it can be stored wrapped in a damp towel in an airtight container for up to a week in the fridge.

BAKED MODELLING DOUGH

- *2 cups of flour*
- *2 tablespoons of vegetable oil*
- *4 teaspoons of cream of tartar*
- *1 cup of salt*
- *2 cups of water*

Put all the ingredients into a saucepan and stir thoroughly. Keep stirring over a low heat for about five minutes until the mixture has thickened into dough. Use the dough to make your models, which can then be placed on a baking tray and cooked in a moderate oven for fifteen minutes.

UNCOOKED MODELLING DOUGH

- *2 cups of flour*
- *1 cup of water*
- *1 cup of powder paint*
- *1 cup of salt*
- *2 tablespoons of vegetable oil*

Mix the ingredients together until all the lumps have been mixed in. Knead the mixture into a ball to make your figurines. The dough will harden as it dries.

VARNISHING YOUR FIGURINE

A white water-based glue is an ideal, safe way to varnish your figurines. This treatment will also strengthen the finished model. Paint the total surface area of your figurine with a layer of glue and leave to dry. If the glue is thick, add water to thin it down. The result is a shiny, strong finish. If you wish to paint your models, apply the paint and then seal with glue. The clay included in this kit is not waterproof. However, if the models are sealed with glue they will be splash-proof and you may set them in a bathroom or outside near a water feature. They should not, though, be left out in heavy rain.

PAINTING YOUR FIGURINE

You can use any water-based paint to colour your figurine. Ordinary powder paint colours from a child's or artist's paint box work well. If you find the paint dries with a chalky appearance, varnish your model with glue, as outlined above, to give a more polished finish. Acrylic paints, watercolour paint, and poster paint also give a satisfying finish.

Although some of the models (the reliefs in particular) may lend themselves to be left unpainted, others come alive with colour and you can make them personalized and unique to you in this way. Some suggestions are listed below of colours that may have been used on the original figurines. You may like to follow these for authenticity.

The top half of the Bird-headed Snake Goddess – from head to hips – can be painted a terracotta colour and the hips and legs with a different colour to indicate her skirt. The original Venus of Laussel has traces of red ochre on her surface, so you could paint her red as she may have been all those years ago, or recreate her appearance today by adding patches of red ochre powder paint to her figure. Isis could be painted a with a mixture of gold and bronze paint to indicate the metallic finish of the original sculpture. The Moroccan Cloth Carder could be painted the terracotta clay colour of the original figurine. The Sleeping Lady of Malta could be painted in a warm pale red and Mary could be painted completely white like those seen in Europe and South America.

Further Techniques

The following techniques can be used to add detail to your figurine, and are included here to give you ideas and inspiration to make each model you make an individual. Feel free to experiment with your own techniques.

MAKING PATTERNS ON THE CLAY

Many buttons have a raised pattern on their front surface; you can experiment by pressing some patterned buttons into a piece of clay. If you like the result use the button technique for the Goddess of Growth's earrings and necklace and on the Moroccan Cloth-Carder's dress. Other household objects could be used to achieve similar results.

STRING

To make a belt or strands of hair you can experiment with cotton thread, wool and string. Press the strand down firmly on to the hair shape, then lift up and pull off. Do the same all the way around the head until you have created a fine head of braided hair.

MATERIAL

To create a texture on the clothing of the figurines simply press a piece of loosely woven cloth like canvas, sack cloth, scrim or muslin on to the surface of your figurine. Press down lightly and ease off using your tool. Do not press too hard; when you peel off the material you should have a textured look.

HANGING UP YOUR MODEL

On completion you may want to hang up your figurine to decorate your walls. Relief carvings, particularly, lend themselves to this treatment. You can make a small hole with a pencil in the middle topside of your relief while the clay is still wet. Knock a small-headed nail or panel pin into the wall. When your relief is fully dry hang it up.

Resources

If you have enjoyed making your goddess and would like to buy extra clay to make the other goddesses featured in this book, the suppliers listed below sell similar air-drying clay which does not need to be fired in a conventional kiln. Similar clays and other media to experiment with are widely available from art shops, toy shops and craft suppliers.

UK

Early Learning Centre
(stores nationwide)
Mail Order from ELC Direct
on 08705 352 352
Order direct from the
website: www.elc.co.uk

AUSTRALIA

Venco Products
29 Owen Road
Kelmscott WA 6111
tel: 61 893995265

USA

Handcraft Designs Inc
63 E. Broad Street
Hatfield
PA 19440
tel: 215 855 3022
fax: 215 855 0184
hdclays@aol.com

Aardvark Clay and Suppliers
1400 East Pomona Street
Santa Ana
CA 92705
tel: 714 541 4157
fax: 714 541 2021

Greatclay
120 South Lincoln Avenue
Carpentersville
Illinois 60110
tel: 800 258 8796
fax: 847 551 1083

CANADA

Cone Art Kilns, Inc.
15 West Pearce Street
77 Richmond Hill
Ontario L4B 1H6
tel: 905 8897 7705

The Pottery Supply House
1120 Speers Road
Oakville, ON
L6L 2X4
800 465 8544
mail@pshcanada.com

Further Reading

Anderson, Jörgen, *The Witch on the Wall*, George Allen & Unwin, 1977.

Anderson, Sarah, *The Virago Book of Spirituality*, Virago Press, 1997.

Atkinson, Clarissa W., Buchanan, Constance H., and Miles, Margaret R., (eds), *Immaculate and Powerful – the Female in Sacred Image and Social Reality*, Beacon Press, 1985.

Baring and Cashford, *The Myth of the Goddess*, Arkana, 1993.

Eck, Dian L., and Jain Devaki, (eds), *Speaking of Faith*, The Women's Press, 1986.

Ehrenberg, Margaret, *Women in Prehistory*, British Museum Press, 1995.

Fisher, Mary Pat, *Living Religions – an Encyclopaedia of the World's Faiths*, I.B.Tauris, 1997.

Garbini, Giovanni *Asian Art* (Myers and Bernard, S., eds), Hamlyn, 1988.

Gimbutas, Marija, *The Goddesses and Gods of Old Europe*, Thames and Hudson Ltd, 1989.

Goodison, Lucy, *Ancient Goddesses and the Myth of Evidence*, British Museum Press, 1998 (published in USA by University of Wisconsin Press, 1999).

Goodison, Lucy, *Moving Heaven and Earth*, Women's Press, 1987.

Graham, Lanier, *Goddesses in Art*, Artabras, 1997.

Green, Miranda, *The Gods of the Celts*, Alan Sutton Publishing Limited, 1986.

Gross, Rita M, *Buddhism after Patriarchy*, State University of New York Press, 1993.

Holden, Pat, (ed.), *Women's Religious Experience: Cross-Cultural Perspectives*, Croom Helm Ltd, 1983.

Iglehart Austin, Hallie, *The House of the Goddess*, Wingbow Press, 1990.

King, Ursula, (ed.), *Women in the World's Religions Past and Present*, Paragon House, 1987.

Larrington, Carolyne, (ed.), *The Woman's Companion to Mythology*, Pandora, 1997.

Long, Asphodel P., *In a Chariot Drawn by Lions*, The Women's Press, 1992.

Mookerjee, Ajit, *Kali and the Feminine Force*, Thames and Hudson, 1998.

Mookerjee, P., *Pathway Icons*, Thames and Hudson Ltd, 1987.

Olson, Carl, *The Book of the Goddess Past and Present*, The Crossroad Publishing Company, 1989.

Radford Reuther, Rosemary, *Woman Guides – Readings toward a Feminist Theology*, Beacon Press, 1985.

Sharma, Arvind (ed), *Women in World Religions*, State University of New York Press, 1987.

Young, Serenity, *Sacred Texts By and About Women*, Pandora, 1993.

Poem on page 37 reproduced from the *Virago Book of Spirituality* (ed. Sarah Anderson). Virago, 1996.

Acknowledgements

Authors' Acknowledgements
The baby poem on page 107 (Akua'ba)
was inspired by and is dedicated to Gabriel,
who was born in London on 1st May 2000,
dangerously premature, and survived.

We are indebted to and would like to
thank the following people, without whom
Create Your Own Goddess would never have
happened. Trudy Harvey for her
groundbreaking work with Sheena in
organizing and leading 'Create Your Own
Goddess' workshops. Carole Grace for
introducing us to each other. Rosi Dodd for
introducing Fran to Elaine Partington and
Liz Wheeler. All past, present and future
participants in 'Create Your Own Goddess'
workshops for keeping alive the art of
female spirituality. The staff and fellow
patrons of the Porchester Spa in London
for maintaining the hot, wet and peaceful
atmosphere in which our conversation
could flourish. And last, but not least,
Jon Bradley and David Edis for being
such nice, loving men.

Eddison•Sadd Editions
Every effort has been made to acknowledge
correctly and contact the source and/or
copyright holder of each picture and piece
of prose or poetry, and Eddison Sadd
Editions apologises for any unintentional
errors or omissions which will be corrected
in future editions of this book.

The *Hymn to Inana* on page 43 is adapted by
Fran Hazelton from *Inana and Iddin-Dagan*
in the Electronic Text Corpus of Sumerian
Literature (www.etcsl.orient.ox.ac.uk)

Anspach Collection, N.Y/Werner Forman
Archive: 102; Brooklyn Museum, N.Y/BAL:
32; Louvre, Paris/BAL: 56; Courtesy © Priya
Mookerjee: 96; Musée d'Aquitaine,
Bordeaux/C.M. Dixon: 26; Musée Guimet,
Paris/Gemeinnützige Stiftung Leonard von
Matt: 84; Musée Guimet, Paris/RMN: 62.
Museum of Cycladic and Ancient Greek Art,
Athens/BAL: 44; Courtesy, National
Museum of the American Indian,
Smithsonian Institution 24/C451. Photo
David Heald: 76; National Museum of
Ireland, Dublin: 90; National Museum,
Valetta/C.M. Dixon: 50; Courtesy of the
Oriental Institute of the University of
Chicago: 38; Roman Museum, Bath: 68.

Special photography by Stephen Marwood.
Special models created by Sheena Barnes
and Eddison Sadd.

Commissioning Editor Liz Wheeler
Editor Nicola Hodgson
Proofreader Jane Struthers
Art Director Elaine Partington
Art Editor Hayley Cove
Picture Researcher Diana Morris
Production Karyn Claridge and
Charles James